PRAISE FOR
THE SURGING TEAM

The Surging Team is a fresh angle on what it takes to be successful in business and life. Scott's holistic approach and thoughtful insights provide the perfect road map to team leadership success.

—DREW GERBER, CEO of Wasabi Publicity, Inc.,
Author of *Destination Aha! Becoming Unstuck in Life and Business*

Scott's message is compelling. I watched him face the challenges at "the large corporation" he cites in the book, and how he always found a way, against odds, to lead his team to deliver the seemingly impossible services being sold by his demanding Director of Marketing. I was that Director of Marketing! Great leadership, Scott!

—MICHAEL DE JONG, former Director of Marketing
at The Signature Group, GE

I have read a lot of business-oriented books over the years. *The Surging Team* was refreshing to me, having been both a small business owner and a corporate person. The building of a work team in any size organization can be a challenge when skill sets and personalities come into play. This is a book and a philosophy that I endorse; it should be followed and embraced!

—DEBI BUSH, Small Business Owner

I recommend this book as a guide to what it takes to thrive in a corporate setting, and how to transfer that same excitement and ethical approach into your own small business.

—GAIL WALLS, Business Owner and Marketing Executive, and Ashland Theological Seminary, Master of Divinity

The Surging Team offers concrete leadership and team building advice for real people. If you're beginning to assume management responsibility in a larger corporation, or interested in starting a small business or opening a franchise location, reading this book could be the best investment you ever make.

—PAUL MISNIAK, Sr. VP at two publicly-traded companies, and Northwestern University MBA, Kellogg Graduate School of Management

I appreciate Scott Brennan's ability to link team success in business to your own personal well-being. This unique approach rings so true; his practical tactics can help lead you to your authentic self and the critical role this plays in leading a high performing team.

—BETH BURNSIDE, Business Owner, and Organizational Learning & Leadership Doctoral Candidate

As a business owner with employees, I'm always looking for ways to motivate and engage them in the business. *The Surging Team* is filled with practical tools on how to do just that and get results. This is a well-written and easy-to-apply guide to team and company success!

—MELISSA AND LENNY KAMMES, Owners of Kammes Colorworks, Inc.

THE SURGING TEAM

THE
Surging
Team

10 BOLDSKILLS^{SM} FOR ACCELERATED TEAM SUCCESS

SCOTT D. BRENNAN

New Insights
PRESS

Published by New Insights Press
Editor: Rick Benzel
Cover and Book Design: Susan Shankin & Associates
Graphics: Tim Kummerow
New Insights Press is an imprint of Over and Above Creative Group
Los Angeles, CA
www.overandabovecreative.com

ISBN: 978-0-9965486-0-1
Library of Congress Control Number: 2015949179

Visit our website and blog for updates: TheSurgingTeam.com

First edition—Printed in the United States of America

This book is dedicated to my wife, Patty.

Throughout this adventure, Patty learned how to best help and love this man of hers, just as John Eldredge wrote about in *Wild at Heart*. "Everybody needs somebody that they can't wait to wake up to and be with each day, and you are my special somebody."

I'll love you forever.

Contents

Acknowledgments   243

About the Author   245

Contact us   247

Introduction

This is a book about learning how to develop and lead a "Surging Team"—a team that demonstrates highly functioning interactive capabilities, achieves seemingly unstoppable momentum, and goes on to accomplish its goals and always win. Surging Teams are full of co-creative drive, pursuing a BOLD purpose, and using collaboration to summon the innovations needed to overcome obstacles. The members of a Surging Team report high levels of emotional well-being, and often describe themselves as "happily getting lost in the flow" of their work. They deeply feel the satisfaction of pursuing their group's BOLD purpose, receiving individual recognition of their unique contributions, and knowing the ultimate gratification of their team's goal achievement. When teams achieve their goals, profits follow.

Years later, team members look back on their Surging Team experience as one that allowed them to truly flourish as individuals—using their unique skills and strengths to a level they never had before. They carry forth their positive feelings about their experience into other things they do and they savor both their personal and team victories. Everyone dreams of doing something they love, while struggling mightily to win, with people they care about. A Surging Team provides a place for each team member to individually flourish while multiplying their efforts as part of a team. They take their Surging Team experience with them into each new future endeavor, and thus become "serial winners."

How do I know about Surging Teams? I know because I have developed and led them. With more than 25 years of experience as a manager, first inside a corporation and later as the owner of my own franchise business, I've been responsible for developing and leading Surging Teams. In my corporate position, building a highly functioning team was driven by necessity and even desperation, as there was simply no way I could achieve my corporate objectives without extraordinary performances by my seemingly ordinary team members. In my franchise business, it became a conscious team-development effort, as I sought to duplicate the team camaraderie and success potential my corporate teams had possessed in the past. In each instance, a Surging Team developed and prospered. Why were my teams able to consistently achieve their goals and win?

The answer lies in one word: **BOLDNESS**. When I worked for a corporation and led my teams, there was a structure, albeit a sometimes adversarial one, that I often had to go around. To succeed in developing and leading a team that was charged with the goal of creating and supporting new products and services, I had to use all the skills and natural ability I possessed as a leader, and some I had not yet fully learned. I negotiated win-win deals with my corporate peers, ignored arbitrary departmental boundaries, and used collaboration to source innovative ideas with my team that we could use to overcome internal and external obstacles. I learned to operate inside our corporate structure as a *bold intrapreneur*—and my teams succeeded.

When I started my franchise business, there was no existing company structure to operate in—only a marketplace that had no tolerance for allowing a new entrepreneur time to learn. Developing a Surging Team under the unforgiving conditions of marketplace competition, and on a limited budget, introduced me to the new and unexpected elements of financial resource deficits and personal pressure. I finally understood that there was a real urgency behind the old adage "time is money." Each hiring or training mistake cost me time, which delayed my drive for breakeven performance and threatened the financial viability of my company.

Financial pressure also conjured a new fear in me—one that had the power to render me nearly immobile at times. Although I was able to develop a successful enterprise, and my franchise business went on to win national awards, quickly achieve breakeven performance, and eventually succeed in a big way—I found that there were periods of time where the financial stress threatened to derail my better judgment. During these times, my former business acumen had to contend with unrelenting financial anxiety. Fortunately, I found that I could hold on to these four sources of hope:

1. The fact that I had a well-thought-out business plan.
2. The knowledge that I'd always been able to win in the past, and I would again if I didn't give up.
3. My belief that I was operating within a larger plan, one with a greater purpose.
4. The confidence that I had as a leader that I could once again develop a Surging Team.

Growing my new business from zero revenues to over one million dollars was a landmark career and personal experience for me. Unfortunately, many of my franchise owner colleagues succumbed to the crucible of franchise anxiety and financial pressure, and their businesses failed.

Building your own unstoppable Surging Team

I wrote this book because it seemed to me that something significant was missing in the literature about team building. It was missing in the many corporate management seminars and workshops
I had been provided, and it was missing in the operations manual
and training that my franchisor had furnished. I knew there had
to be a more reliably repeatable methodology to build an unstoppable Surging Team—before the intrapreneur succumbed to the
pressure of corporate norms, and before the entrepreneur's financial fears triumphed—but I could not find such a book.

The classic books on entrepreneurship provide a few insights on
team building—books like *The E-Myth, Good to Great, Think and Grow
Rich, The Greatest Salesman in the World, The Seven Habits of Highly
Effective People, Selling with Noble Purpose,* as well as biographies
of leaders like Theodore Roosevelt, George Washington, Abraham
Lincoln, Ulysses S. Grant, and the enigmatic Steve Jobs. But, while
fascinating, these books don't directly explain how to reliably
and repeatedly build, nurture, and lead an effective, unstoppable
team—regardless of the type of organization you're working in.

In my view, most current literature seems focused on "hiring
the best people" and "getting rid of those who don't fit," not on
developing normal humans and nurturing the conditions for your
team to succeed. I felt there had to be a better way than adopting a
methodology that revolved around constantly searching for the "A
players," evaluating your team members, purging those who no
longer fit, replacing them with new team members, training them,
and then starting the exhausting cycle over again. Any leader
charged with managing this endless cycle of "talent purging and
replenishment" would soon become weary of leading—and would
certainly not describe their role as allowing people to "flourish."

Despite many existing management books, much of what
I read focused on theory, but I needed something I could apply right

now in my business. There seemed room for a book that specifically addressed how business leaders can reliably and repeatedly build highly effective, flourishing teams from seemingly ordinary people—especially teams that are charged with accomplishing goals that require innovation and creativity in order to succeed. This new book would need to explain how to lead this team in an unstoppable mission of surging past any internal or external success barriers, and on to achieve its goals.

The job expectations and social needs held by today's workers—combined with the critical marketplace importance of a team that refuses to quit—require a complex, sensitive, and empowering team environment. Building this group, which I call the Surging Team, deserves a book dedicated to offering the team leader a blueprint to follow, one that allows individual team members to flourish, while consistently accomplishing company goals. This new book must be a resource to help a team leader or business owner in the current moment to overcome immediate success obstacles.

The Surging Team is the result of my commitment to make such a methodology available to many. The key to this book is what I have come to call BOLDskills for Accelerated Team Success. I have laid out 10 specific BOLDskills a leader must learn and then master in order to quickly achieve *reliably repeatable* team success. These skills create and nurture the delicate and elusive conditions whereby astounding team success can emerge. By keeping team members fulfilled in their work—crafting for each of them engrossing experiences of engagement in their objectives—a team leader will be able to keep his team together, supporting each other through all the human struggles they have professionally and personally, so that the team can quickly and reliably achieve their objectives.

With these BOLDskills, the distraction of identifying and replacing "non-performers" and then identifying and hiring replacements will be greatly reduced. The time and energy gained by this shift in the management process can be better spent finding innovative ways to achieve your objectives. My paradigm helps keep a team intact because the individual members place great value on maintaining their common feelings of engagement and collective spirit. When this occurs, even a competing job offer with greater compensation does not necessarily entice someone who is experiencing the intangible benefits of a job that she considers a significant source of happiness and well-being, and allows her to pursue a worthy objective.

It is through repeated team success that your entrepreneurial business or your corporate division will smash through internal and external barriers. I've worked on successful corporate teams, led corporate teams, and then started my own franchise business and created and led a successful team. My teams often won the top honors that my company or industry had to offer. But the honors were not my goal or our team's goal—we just wanted to succeed. Others who appreciated our "audacity of winning" provided the honors. This book was written to help you and your team win, and to accelerate your success.

Who will benefit from reading this book?

This book is for anyone, whether an entrepreneur in your own business or a leader in a corporate environment, who will be leading a team of at least five people. I use five team members as the starting point for considering our BOLDskills methodology, because it's around that number when a leader begins to lose control of effectively managing their team of unique individuals, and is open to adopting a formal team-building methodology. The sheer magnitude of the cost represented by the combined team members' compensation, along with the difficulty of the management effort, and the seemingly unending team recruitment cycle—are all reaching a crescendo at about five team members. This threshold is when there is definitely a felt need for intentional and coherent team-building, based on sound team management principles and a success system. Without such a methodology, the team starts to lose focus, and precious emotional energy is spent "fixing team problems" instead of remaining focused on achieving objectives.

This need for skills mastery to reliably and repeatedly build a Surging Team is especially important for teams that will at times need to use radically innovative thinking in order to achieve complex objectives. Whether you're an entrepreneur building your own business, or an intrapreneur leading a corporate team that must creatively use company resources to achieve your team goals—if your success depends on the ability of your team to consistently and creatively overcome obstacles, then you need the BOLDskills for Accelerated Team Success methodology outlined in this book.

A note for intrapreneurs

I define *intrapreneur* as someone who is not an actual company owner, but is rather a professional manager or senior subject-matter expert charged with managing and leading highly effective internal teams within multi-department organizations. Most professional managers have little or no training in team building, and are left without practical guidance in two of the most challenging arenas the business world provides—human motivation and team success. Like me, many corporate managers come from the ranks of professional engineers or subject-matter experts. Having demonstrated expert technical skills, they're often promoted by their organization to lead a group of their former peers.

However, many skilled engineers and professionals are unable to successfully make the transition to effective leadership. The linear progression of a team's success is not simply a mathematical measurement achieved by extrapolating the combined value of the team's individual knowledge resources. Many of us have had encounters with such dysfunctional team leaders, who were and may still be skilled engineers. Our BOLDskills for Accelerated Team Success are designed to provide effective "accelerated" access to a methodology of team success for such managers who are taking on a leadership role.

A note for entrepreneurs

The *entrepreneur*, the owner of an innovative small to medium-sized company, has a slightly different dynamic at play that makes accelerated team success even more urgent. That dynamic is *scarcity*—the scarcity of financial resources and the emotional capacity of the entrepreneurial owner to deal with all the challenges a new company faces. If an entrepreneur runs out or just gets close to running out of either resource, bad things start to happen. The more quickly the entrepreneur can build and motivate a Surging Team—a team that's able to consistently achieve company success goals—the more likely she'll be able to focus her energy on the strategies needed to reach the financial breakeven point and relieve the pressure. That is where healthy "work-life balance" lives for the entrepreneur. Once the company breakeven line is crossed, the owner develops a new feeling of peace and accomplishment and can begin to enjoy the fruits of successful business ownership. Our BOLDskills for Accelerated Team Success methodology is designed to accelerate the entrepreneur's attainment of this work-life balance.

The 10 BOLD Skills for Accelerated Team Success— Our BOLDskills

As described above, I've had the unique experience of developing and leading unstoppable Surging Teams in both the intrapreneurial and entrepreneurial environments. Having succeeded in both arenas, though at times with great trepidation and no substantial guidance, I acquired a keen interest in creating a reliably repeatable methodology for quickly building successful teams. My learnings became the BOLDskills for Accelerated Team Success that are explained in this book.

Overall, this book was written to give you, the company owner or the professional manager, the tools and reliably repeatable process to transform your company's employees or departmental staff into an unstoppable Surging Team. I want you to feel the power of the collective spirit of your team as you lead them to achieve seemingly impossible goals. Some of those goals include financial success, revenue multiples, new product launches, and work-life freedom. Your team members will never forget their powerfully positive experience with you as leader of their Surging Team, and each one will benefit both professionally and personally from their participation in the team. As the professional manager or company owner, you will also attain a level of well-being that you likely did not expect, because you will share in the flourishing of individuals who are pursuing the mutually desirable goals of their team. When work teams flourish, increased profits will follow. This miracle, the power of a Surging Team, is available to those who dream, and then dare greatly.

About Scott Brennan

I will be citing numerous examples in the forthcoming chapters reflecting my business experience, so I want to provide some context so you can understand them better.

One of my experiences was being the leader of a "skunk-works" team for a division of a GE company. While I was doing this, I was also working on an MBA in the evenings. This gave me a fantastic opportunity to apply what I was learning in class immediately—in fact, the very next day with my team. Several years later, I was fortunate to be there to see the results of my team-building efforts. In the midst of a whirlwind time at GE, I was awarded the "Chairman's Challenge Award for Outstanding Intrapreneur-ship," an award I didn't even know existed. I hadn't realized how rare it is for a large company, a corporation, to innovate a new service or create a new product, successfully introduce it into the marketplace, and have the marketplace recognize it as valuable and desirable. But in retrospect, I keenly appreciate the rarity of a successful innovative process.

After leaving that corporate career, I was naturally lured by entrepreneurship—owning and building my own company. My belief was that my intrapreneurship experience had predisposed me for success in this related arena. I purchased and was able to grow a franchise IT service business from zero to over $1 million in revenue, before selling it profitably. But the process of growing my own company was far more challenging than I was prepared for. The urgency felt by an entrepreneur with limited personal re-sources was enough to drive me to the edge of solvency and sanity. But it was there, at the edge of my abilities, that I learned the most about what the entrepreneur needs to do to succeed—quickly build an unstoppable Surging Team. Along the way to my success as an entrepreneur, I was awarded both the coveted "Franchise of the Year" and the "Million Dollar Club" awards. In this new arena of entrepreneurship, my team had succeeded, and my interest in creating a reliably repeatable methodology for developing and leading an unstoppable Surging Team only increased.

After selling my franchise business, and having the work-life freedom to spend a season reflecting on these experiences, I no-ticed there were striking similarities in how I achieved success with my teams in both the corporate environment and in the small business environment. Some of the success techniques came from my corporate experience, some from what I learned in my grad-uate MBA program, and some from my hard-won knowledge in the crucible of urgency and accountability that is running a small business.

I believe that the same skills needed by an entrepreneur are also needed by the corporate team leaders and managers responsible for the success of their company teams or divisions. This is especially the case for intrapreneurs leading teams charged with attaining outcomes that depend on summoning innovation and creativity. I began to document these skills and they became the BOLDskills for Accelerated Team Success that you will learn in this book.

These 10 BOLDskills are designed to guide a team leader in immediately applying a reliably repeatable methodology designed to nurture the conditions for a Surging Team to emerge, conditions that will propel their team beyond internal and external obstacles and on to ultimate success in achieving their objectives. The common thread of success in my experience is finding a way to quickly build thriving teams from ordinary people, and allowing each team member to flourish and contribute far beyond the sum of their expected individual contributions.

After reading this book, I hope that you—team leaders and company owners—will be motivated to transform your company or your department into an unstoppable Surging Team—a team that refuses to quit, until they win. That is what I want for my readers.

Scott Brennan
President & Accelerated Success Expert,
BOLDbreak, Inc.

What is a Surging Team?

Our greatest weakness lies in giving up. The most certain way to succeed is always to try just one more time.
—THOMAS EDISON

"How the heck did you do that?" Bill, our VP of Information Technology (IT), asked me after calling me into his office. I had a pretty good idea what he was talking about.

It was just a few weeks prior that I had to pick up one of my team members, Dale, because his car wouldn't start. His house was cluttered, and several of his small children were getting ready for school. They needed their daddy, but my corporate skunk-works team needed him too. His wife thanked me for coming to pick him up, and we headed off for work to complete our system prototype.

Giving him a lift wasn't just me being nice. Our system prototype wasn't finished yet, and Dale was our team's computer programmer. Time was running out. The Senior VP hadn't given us much of a budget, so I'd assembled a small team of some ordinary people, normal people like Dale with real life problems and obligations beyond work—people we could afford to hire. With this team of ordinary people, we had to create a working prototype with the few company resources we were given. If not, then the effort would be deemed a failure, and if we were lucky, we'd all be re-assigned somewhere else in the organization. If we weren't lucky, we'd lose our jobs.

I had previously worked on Bill's IT computer applications development team, until I was recruited by the marketing department to head up this new skunk-works project. Marketing needed an exciting new restaurant product to keep the interest of our major clients—some airline companies—and they needed it *now*. They weren't exactly sure what the new product was supposed to do, but it had to involve eating at great restaurants and then getting either a cash discount or, better yet, a dining reward that could be translated into receiving airline miles. My job was to figure out what could be done—and how to make it work. Marketing had made a promise to their clients, and now we had a deadline.

There had been some tension between Bill and me over this project. He suspected that I was using my "insider" IT knowledge from working with him before, in order to get more of the company's computing resources than he deemed my skunk-works project "deserved to get." A few weeks ago, he had "drawn the line" and refused to engage his programming staff any further in my skunk-works product development effort. I was "eating up his resources," he claimed. So I had to rely solely on the talent of my own team members and hiring a motivated outsourcing vendor in order to replace the loss of Bill's professional computer programming staff.

Now four months later, I was sitting across from his desk, and Bill was staring at a rebate award for his own recent dining event at a nearby, participating restaurant. He was stunned that we were able to track his personal dining by monitoring his credit card, produce a rebate, and do it in time to meet marketing's deadline—without *his* IT department's help.

"How the heck did you do that, Scott?" Bill repeated. "I can't believe it."

I couldn't give him the answer, because I didn't yet understand that I'd built an unstoppable Surging Team.

Surging Teams produce innovations,
have higher productivity, and lower turnover

Where does innovation come from? Do we need to wait for a genius to be born like Einstein, Edison, Ford, or Steve Jobs? Or can innovation be summoned whenever it's needed if we have the foresight and skills to carefully set the conditions? I believe the latter is true.

Surging Teams that are made up of ordinary people, led by a skilled leader, are incubators for innovation. In the face of success obstacles, Surging Teams are able to identify known best-practices and, if needed, produce innovative solutions that allow the team to quickly and creatively navigate around barriers that prevent successful goal achievement. But how?

Innovations emerge when the known best practices are recognized as insufficient to overcome the current obstacles—and when the key team elements of goal urgency, clear accountability, member well-being, a BOLD purpose, and a spirit of entrepreneurial collaboration take over to discover a new best practice. The team that has these key elements can use peer brainstorming techniques (which we'll discuss later in this book) to generate innovative ideas that the team leader can decide to use in order to achieve a goal.

What I've learned is that having a Surging Team is a key to unlocking innovation. We're all born with a different combination of strengths and talents. One thing we have in common, however, is that we're social creatures. We're at our best when working as part of a group, and jointly accountable to achieve a BOLD goal, one that's beyond the ability of any single person to achieve. Think of the movie "Apollo 13." It took a significant team of people, all with different skills, but all with a common BOLD goal—to assure that the Apollo 13 astronauts returned safely from their mission. We all long to be an important part of something noble, something larger than ourselves. That is when we flourish as humans.

If you have ever studied psychology, you know Maslow's hierarchy of human needs places "self-actualization" at the top of its pyramid—the equivalent of "flourishing." We reach this top-of-the-pyramid level when our work allows us to invoke our creativity, spontaneity, and problem solving—and to do this with the respect of others who appreciate our efforts and who are similarly engaged in flourishing in a coordinated group effort to achieve a mutual, worthy and BOLD goal.

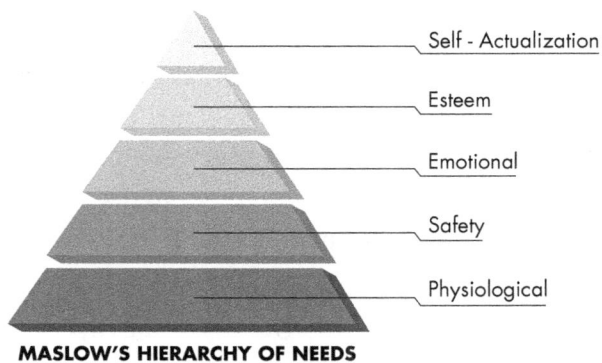

Self - Actualization

Esteem

Emotional

Safety

Physiological

MASLOW'S HIERARCHY OF NEEDS

Have you ever been part of a Surging Team? You'd remember it if you were. It's an experience that you cherish, smile about, and sometimes laugh out loud whenever you remember a story about the team. That's because a Surging Team depends on each member to individually flourish and contribute to a mighty, collective effort to achieve a worthy and BOLD goal. When teams reach the Surging Team level, they feel unstoppable, and they somehow find a way to achieve their objectives—on time and within budget.

Companies should embrace Surging Teams, because they are a major factor in retaining successful employees and ultimately in driving company profits. When given a choice of working on a Surging Team, or making more money at a less fulfilling job, people tend to choose the more fulfilling job—and those who choose the higher pay job soon regret their choice. Higher pay is a jail sentence if the work is not fulfilling. A Surging Team allows individuals to flourish and develop increased levels of well-being and productiv-ity, while the team achieves its market-driven goals. This compo-nent of developing individual well-being functions as a cohesive glue that binds each team member to the team, trusting others, so she can then unreservedly commit her personal resources to the team's objectives. This individual well-being component dramati-cally reduces team turnover and hastens the development of Surg-ing Team qualities.

Of course, the most blatant reason that a company should em-brace the intentional development of Surging Teams is that they have higher productivity. Members of a Surging Team are able to sustain longer periods of engagement in their work, often referred to as "flow." During periods of flow, people are using their most highly developed "signature strengths" to work on their tasks. They often report losing track of time and feeling either that "time seemed to stop" or that "time flew by."

By leveraging this high level of engagement, a Surging Team is able to consistently perform at optimum speed and creativity, achieve objectives, and do their job while remaining on schedule and within budget. A large company comprised of Surging Teams will maximize the value of its human resource investment. An en-trepreneur with just a small staff will maximize the value of his cadre of workers. In both cases, the result is goal achievement, a highly engaged workforce, and higher profitability.

Would you describe your company or your corporate team as a Surging Team?

Take this assessment to gauge your team's Surging Team Success profile. If you are the team leader, answer the questions for your-self as if you are a team member, and then give it to each member of your team. It is designed to be taken by each team member to help you assess their opinions, too.

THE SURGING TEAM PROFILE ASSESSMENT

	Surging Team Profile Assessment Questions	No	Maybe	Yes
1.	Does each member of your team understand what their shared BOLD purpose is?			
2.	Do you trust your direct team leader, whether it's the business owner, or another executive?			
3.	Do you believe that your team will overcome all obstacles and eventually succeed?			
4.	Has your team innovated creative ways to get around problems and obstacles?			
5.	Is each team member included in the planning process to set the team's objectives?			
6.	Does your team always achieve its objectives?			
7.	Does your team leader ask for and implement ideas proposed by the team members?			
8.	Do you feel that there is a direct link between your individual efforts on the team, and the success of the team?			
9.	Are your team members able to overcome the drama in their personal lives, so they can work effectively?			
10.	Is your team leader effective in resolving both internal and external conflict that impedes your team's success?			
11.	Is quitting your job unimaginable?			
12.	Have you experienced extended periods of engagement, or "being in the flow" while working?			
13.	Do you feel a powerfully positive collective spirit when your team is together?			
14.	Does your team have stories they tell that demonstrate their positive collective spirit, and the team's BOLD purpose?			
15.	Is your company achieving high levels of profitability?			
	Total number in each category			

If your "Yes" scores are greater than your "No" scores, then your team is on the way to becoming an unstoppable Surging Team. If you have at least 11 "Yes" scores, then your team is already displaying multiple Surging Team characteristics and your team leader is doing a good job. If you gave this survey out to your team members, tally their scores and calculate the average total in each category. As the company owner or team leader, your goal is to improve the combined Surging Team profile "Yes" scores of your team members, and we can help you can get there!

You can also use feedback from these two additional questions in your assessment. Have your team members write a few paragraphs to respond to each of these questions:

- Describe how it feels to be part of our team.
- What would help our team perform better?

Review their statements and take seriously what your team members tell you. Hold onto these statements for future reference and comparison.

5 characteristics of Surging Teams

These are the characteristics of a Surging Team:

1. Is made up of ordinary people, with a shared BOLD purpose
2. Has a leader they trust
3. Believes they'll always win, and are permanently imprinted by success
4. Innovates ways around all internal and external obstacles and refuses to give up
5. Always meets their objectives, on time, and within budget

Everyone wants to be part of a team that wins. Most of us long to be recognized for our contributions and accepted as valued team members. Is it an accident to be part of a wildly successful team?

Some people have never experienced a Surging Team, so it seems like luck or the confluence of random events to be part of one. I strongly contend that creating a Surging Team is an intentional phenomenon, and can be achieved using a reliably repeatable methodology like our BOLDskills for Accelerated Team Success.

The high cost of not building a Surging Team

I've seen deception, backstabbing, skullduggery and even embezzlement happen on teams that others led and I was a member of—and that's only the instances I've been aware of. I've also been a member of mediocre teams that either didn't have specific objectives or whose objectives were purposefully subjective and unmeasurable. Some of my former corporate team leaders tried to limit their ability to be held accountable, so that the attainment of success and "bonuses or at least a raise" could be gained through a subjective and passionately delivered argument. Have you seen the movie "Office Space?" I always had the sense that a member of my former corporate computer programming department produced that movie. On these types of teams, at least the criminal drama can be entertaining, for a while, but it is not the work environment most people desire.

Team leaders who deliberately or incompetently set a very low bar for team success are not acknowledging a basic human need: *people long to be led and desire to be part of a seemingly impossible mission.* Failing to understand this, their teams do indeed develop their own challenging objectives, but those are too often illegal or counter to company culture. Members of a corporate team that is not surging—that has no daunting challenge to tackle together—can't wait to quit, find other "drama" to get involved in, and only hang on long enough to find another job. I know; I've been on such teams. What a waste of company resources and human potential.

If you're a member of a team that doesn't have a BOLD purpose and difficult objectives—ones that challenge and inspire you—don't wait; get out of there as fast as you can and save your career, your self-worth, and maybe even your marriage. If you hang on, it will insidiously affect you and dull your talent until you feel that you're just hiding out at your job and hoping nobody finds out that you're "not doing much of any importance." What a waste of your life.

BOLD Takeaways

- Members of a Surging Team report increased feelings of well-being as well as experiencing extended periods of engagement while working on their tasks. They are often lost "in the flow" of their work. These outcomes ultimately result in higher productivity and profitability.

- Each member of a Surging Team is permanently imprinted by being in the crucible of a shared BOLD struggle. Each member leverages their savored team victory into many subsequent career wins. They believe they will always succeed, and each becomes a serial winner. They never forget what it felt like to work on a Surging Team, one that valued their unique contributions.

- Characteristics of a Surging Team:
    1. Is made up of ordinary people, with a shared BOLD purpose
    2. Has a leader they trust
    3. Believes they'll always win, and are permanently imprinted by success
    4. Innovates ways around all internal and external obstacles and refuses to give up
    5. Always meets their objectives, on time, and within budget

- Surging Teams experience lower turnover of staff, even when higher compensating jobs are available from competitors. The feelings of well-being and happiness experienced by members of a Surging Team are many times more valuable than incremental increases in compensation.

- Surging Teams are able to source innovative ideas in order to get past a success obstacle. It will be up to the team leader to decide if one of these innovative ideas will need to be used in order to achieve the team's goal—on time and within budget.

Introducing BOLDskills for Accelerated Team Success

Act boldly and unseen forces will come to your aid.
— DOROTHEA BRANDE

"What should I be working on?" I asked my manager, Jang. It had been a few days since I started this new computer programming job, and I was becoming uncomfortable not doing much of anything so far.

"Just read through the code of a few of our computer programs for now," said Jang. He then pointed to a bookshelf that contained some printed versions of our company's most critical software.

"Is there a particular problem with any of these programs I should be looking for?" I asked, trying to narrow down this quixotic and mind-numbing task. Each program contained thousands of lines of code.

"Just read them and let me know when you're done," Jang said. "Take the first one now and he again pointed up to the top shelf at a six-inch thick printed copy of computer programming "source code."

"Ok, I'll get to work on it," I agreed, and I took the program and went back to my cubicle.

Two weeks later, I returned to Jang's office. "I think I found a way to improve the main billing program," I said a little excitedly.

"What do you mean?" asked Jang, a little startled.

I lifted up the printed copy of the program as I began to explain, "I think I found a way to improve the speed of the main billing subroutine when it runs each night," but Jang looked confused and cut me off with a wave of his hand.

"There is no problem with the billing program," he said, "I just wanted you to get familiar with how it was written. Please leave it here now and take the next one," he said, again pointing to the bookshelf.

As I walked back to my cubicle, I wondered how other people in the computer programming department were dealing with their own boredom. Some were talking on the phone, or gathered in "meetings" that were really just fun conversations. There seemed to be no mutually important purpose that we were coming to achieve each day. We were all just waiting for somebody to assign us some new programming to do. I began to hate my work life, and it didn't have to be that way.

BOLDskills for Accelerated Team Success is born

The above true story was one of many I experienced as a member of a corporate computer programming staff. It opened my eyes to how much time, money, and human potential are wasted when a company promotes someone from the ranks of their professional technical staff—but then provides them with little or no management training. Jang was a kind and intelligent man, but he was not an inspirational nor effective team leader.

Over the years, there were many opportunities on the various computer programming teams I was on to engage the team members, give them a BOLD purpose, and allow them to flourish.

Business issues that needed attention and would have benefited from some BOLD leadership included:

- An unending list of requests for computer support by the other company departments
- Monitoring the success of the computer programs as they updated customer records
- Effective oversight and debriefing of the staff assigned to "weekend on-call duty"
- Skill enhancement for team members to prepare for transitions to the next generation of computer system tools

But our managers had recently been senior technicians themselves, and they didn't know how to create an environment where team members were able to flourish. How could they quickly acquire some tools to help them successfully motivate and lead their teams? There seemed to be no time to send our team leaders to "management training." They had to learn these skills on-the-job, but the more likely result was to never to learn them at all. These technical managers usually defaulted to "if it isn't broken, then don't fix it" as their management principle. If that meant that we often had little to do (even as our team leader stalled the snow-balling requests for computer support), then so be it.

Managers in the non-technical departments weren't any better at creating an environment where we were encouraged to flourish. "Lying low," following procedures, and avoiding embarrassing screw-ups was their management mantra. If we screwed up while following procedures, at least we had plausible deniability and could blame the procedures for unwanted outcomes or shortcomings.

Over time and through many such experiences, it occurred to me that the real need was *more effective training for team leaders.* The company needed team development training that could be imparted within a very short period of time—training that would be received as a valued expansion of the team leader's management and leadership skills. We needed leaders who could inspire us to understand our strengths and solicit our ideas in pursuit of a mutually-held and worthy goal. When a company eventually realizes that their leaders need these skills, they want them taught and learned quickly—right now. That's what our BOLDskills are designed to do: accomplish *Accelerated* Team Success.

I've been on work teams that underperformed or failed, but I have also repeatedly led teams that wildly succeeded. "What made the difference?" I began wondering. My own team success experiences both inside a corporate structure and then within my own business intrigued me. How can a company avoid the colossal waste of human potential and company resources that a dysfunctional team and ineffective team leader often delivers?

This question seemed worth some thoughtful effort. I examined the over-the-top, multi-year, serial team success experiences I'd led, with the goal of answering the question: "How can a team leader repeatedly inspire a team of workers to achieve astounding success, to become a Surging Team?"

Through personal experiences like the one above, BOLDskills for Accelerated Team Success was born. BOLDskills is a comprehensive program designed to close the gap between the need for timely and effective team leadership and management skills, and the common training (or lack thereof) that most managers get. It also answers the related questions, "How can our managers quickly gain valued skills, which allow them to succeed in leading effective teams?" and the follow-up question, "How do we know if the training was truly effective?" Lastly, it offers insights into the origins of and the strategic summoning and use of innovation by a team. This book offers a broad, creative, and effective response to answer the above questions.

Both entrepreneurs and intrapreneurs need BOLDskills

I presented earlier a compelling case for the needs of both *entrepreneurial* business owners and *intrapreneurial* corporate team leaders to learn how to develop Surging Teams. This is especially true for leaders of teams that need to use creativity and innovation to achieve their goals. The BOLDskills for Accelerated Team Success methodology is the foundation for how to build Surging Teams, and is equally relevant in both environments.

I know from experience that the forces aligned against innovative behavior emerging from inside a larger company are so great, that a team leader who attempts to embrace intrapreneurial tactics to achieve breakthrough success will continually fear for his career. To counteract this, you need an "edge" to navigate past the formidable corporate forces that compel adherence to the "operations manual" and the "keep your head down and don't make waves" school of management. I know.

The BOLDskills for Accelerated Team Success was designed to provide you, the innovative team leader, that edge, by providing a reliably repeatable method to transform your team into an unstoppable Surging Team, a team that defeats all internal and external obstacles on the way to achieving its objectives. These skills must be learned and mastered by you, the team leader, in order for a business or a corporate team to succeed. However, they are not widely or effectively taught in colleges or business graduate programs, and they are only randomly or incompletely learned through life or traditional career experience. Most of our universities are ineffective in closing this team leadership skills gap, which is indeed an international need. These skills are usually only learned under extreme duress by the owner of a business or by the manager of a corporate team—when urgency is high, accountability is clear, and a team effort is needed to win. These are extremely difficult circumstances in which to learn how to effectively lead a team.

Most people thrust into leadership positions do not learn team management skills quickly enough, and the underlying reason for many corporate team and business failures is directly related to this issue. The fastest way to take advantage of the power of the BOLDskills methodology is by learning it in advance of being needed, and then systematically mastering these skills. This means training new managers early on in their careers.

However, the BOLDskills methodology can also be brought in as soon as a company recognizes that the leadership skills of their current managers and executives need to be upgraded—and in a hurry. Symptoms of this need include inopportune or increasing departures of key team members, leaders who regularly miss key deliverable dates, and chronic project cost overruns. Each of these events is extremely costly for a large company—and potentially the cause of the financial or operational collapse of a smaller company. I've seen both, up close and personal.

Even if you earned an MBA, or have a relevant management degree, your education likely did not have a focus on applied team development, especially on teams that must consistently summon and use innovation in order to achieve their goals. Many colleges are of little help to their students when it comes to addressing the stunning lack of entrepreneurial and intrapreneurial leadership training. Most colleges are still teaching coursework designed to serve a pre-2008 economy, and are not training a new generation of innovators, leaders, and entrepreneurs for today's world. This lack of bold entrepreneurial and intrapreneurial leadership training, combined with increasing need for innovation and new ideas in the business world, is contributing to widespread leadership skills ignorance. Forbes Magazine recently predicted that "50-80% of new businesses will fail within the first 3 years." Many businesses never get beyond start-up, and others, if they survive, never generate sufficient net income to provide for the work-life balance needs of the owner. That is not success.

Anyone in a team leadership position, who doesn't have training in team leadership skills or the desire to acquire that training—will put their team at serious risk of failure. It's so critical to a company to have an inspired and highly trained team leadership pipeline, that anyone filling a leadership position who does not have or is not trying to acquire effective team management skills—should be immediately replaced with someone who will.

The BOLDskills for Accelerated Team Success provides every team leader an invaluable toolbox of the skills needed to enable and inspire your team to achieve its objectives and become an unstoppable Surging Team—a team where each member is encouraged to flourish and contribute to its goals.

The 10 BOLDskills for Accelerated Team Success

The rest of the chapters in this book will examine in detail, one by one, the 10 critical team leadership success skills contained in our BOLDskills for Accelerated Team Success program. It was designed for you, the soon-to-be BOLD team leader or company owner, as a reliably repeatable methodology to develop and lead your Surging Team. To give you an overview, the 10 BOLDskills are:

1. Learn and then adopt the BOLD Success Principle
2. Always use a formal business plan and include your team in the process
3. Identify and adopt a BOLD purpose
4. Provide ownership engagement, inspired leadership, and trusted management
5. BOLDLY work to increase the positive collective spirit of your team
6. Hire or fire according to strategic goals, not out of panic or convenience

7. Practice win-win negotiation in all spheres of your business relationships
8. Make peace with fear and doubt, as they are constant companions of leaders
9. Become a BOLD salesperson for your business, and your team
10. Lay the groundwork for the profitable future sale of your business or division

BOLD Takeaways

- Many team leaders were very recently senior technicians themselves, and don't know how to create an environment where their team members are able to flourish. "Lying low," following procedures and avoiding embarrassing screw-ups is a popular but misguided management mantra.

- It's so critical to a company to have inspired and trained team leadership that anyone filling a leadership position who does not have, or is not trying to acquire, effective team leadership and management skills should be immediately replaced with someone who will.

- Effective team leadership skills are not reliably taught in schools at any level or learned through life or casual career experience. They're usually learned only under extreme duress by the owner of a business or the leader of a corporate team, by confronting the many internal and external obstacles to success in their "crucible of urgency and accountability." Most people leading a business team do not learn these skills quickly enough, and the underlying reason for their team's failure to achieve its objectives is directly linked to this oversight.

- The BOLDskills for Accelerated Team Success methodology was designed to provide you, the innovative team leader, with a reliably repeatable method to transform your team into an unstoppable Surging Team—one that defeats all internal and external obstacles to achieve its objectives.

- Surging Teams are able to summon and use innovation in order to overcome success obstacles. This is a skill that is difficult to replicate, and it gives a significant marketplace edge to a Surging Team.

BOLDskill 1

Learn and Adopt the
BOLD Success Principle

If opportunity doesn't knock, build a door.
— MILTON BERLE

"Come in, Scott," said the Senior Vice President of product development. "Have a seat."

I was a little intimidated. Jane had a reputation of having a short temper and being generally disagreeable, but she made me feel comfortable as I sat down.

"So, tell me what's on your mind?" Jane invited.

Getting right to the point, I jumped in with both feet. "The Director of Marketing is selling services that we don't have and asking me to find a way to deliver those services." I paused to see how this information was being received.

"Go on," Jane encouraged me.

"I think he's putting our division at risk by demanding that I find a way to support services that we don't have and can't deliver to our customers." That was my message, so I assumed a countenance of having finished and waited for her response.

"You're the Director of Operations, right?" Jane confirmed.

"Yes," I verified, unknowingly falling right into her trap.

Jane put the palms of her hands on her desk and slowly raised all 5' 5" of herself up. She leaned over into my space, and yelled into my face, "THEN DIRECT!"

The shock on my face must have been priceless. My lips quivered, but no words formed. Jane didn't flinch; she just continued to stare me down. My only options were to quietly leave her office and find a way to deal with the marketing director, or to quit, and both scenarios ran through my head. I decided to quietly leave her office.

It took me a few weeks to realize what I'd learned, though during that time I drafted my letter of resignation and kept it in my pocket, daring myself each day to quit and simmering with outrage over how I was treated. As I searched for empathy, a senior executive friend of mine did not have the same reaction as I did. He suggested that "Jane may have lacked tact, but maybe there was some *truth* to her advice." I rejected his assessment.

But oddly enough, out of the clear blue sky, I received an unsolicited mailing at my home, from a Christian organization that I was not a member of, which contained this Bible verse from John 8:32:

" . . . *and you will know the truth, and the truth will set you free."*

As I read the words, my first thought was that my executive friend was trying to play a joke on me—since his advice and the random mailing had the exact same message about "truth." However, I had to discard this possibility, as there was no way he could have gotten a mailing to me so quickly after our discussion. As I considered this coincidence, I suddenly realized what I needed to accept. It was my job as the Director of Operations to either secure the company's resources and find a way to deliver the services being sold by our Director of Marketing, or negotiate with him to make sure we both agreed on what was possible to deliver.

In an instant, my outrage vanished, and I tore up my resigna-tion notice. It became crystal clear that this was an opportunity to develop my leadership and my team's success potential. I made it my mission to figure out a way for my department to deliver on the wild service claims being made. I also realized that some-body really wanted me to learn this lesson, a lesson in opportunity awareness and leadership. I still have that unsolicited mailing.

Two years after my encounter with Sr. VP Jane, I received the "Chairman's Challenge Award for Outstanding Intrapreneurship" from our company's notorious Chairman of the Board, an award I had no idea even existed.

The BOLD Success Principle for leaders of a Surging Team

The lessons learned from that abrupt lesson in executive leader-ship and opportunity awareness have influenced me ever since. There is no perfect team success opportunity, only ordinary ones disguised as problems. Don't shy away from or complain about seemingly impossible challenges; they may turn out to be success opportunities in disguise.

Malcolm Gladwell, in his book *Outliers: The Story of Success,* has a fascinating thought on where success comes from. He writes, "...success follows a predictable course. It's not the brightest who succeed ... [but rather] those who have been given opportu-nities—and who have the presence of mind to seize them."

Notice Gladwell did not say "those who have been given *per-fect* opportunities." Aren't we all given opportunities in life and in business? Are any of them perfect? He also uses the verb "to seize." This is a rather violent action, seizing something—much bolder than "asking." But that's what you must do if you want success—you must *seize an ordinary opportunity* for yourself.

So with deference to Gladwell, his saying inspired me to recog-nize what I call our BOLD Success Principle:

Success follows a predictable course. It's not the brightest who
succeed, or those presented with a perfect opportunity.
Success follows those who have been given ordinary opportunities—
and who have the presence of mind and the courage to seize them.

My reasoning is that in order to be bold enough to seize something, you have to have courage—and something to seize. You can wait your entire life for the perfect opportunity to show up—and it may never arrive. Instead, if you really want success, you must resolve to gather your courage and seize an ordinary opportunity for yourself and your team. You need to recognize these as "team success opportunities."

How can I learn to improve my opportunity awareness?

"Opportunity awareness" is the awareness of the team leader to identify team success opportunities that he can then use to engage his team in, and thereby develop the team's success potential. How do you develop this capability?

In my experience and through research on human behavior, I believe I have discovered one of the most important factors to help leaders develop greater awareness capacities—it's done by increasing your own happiness and well-being as the team leader or company owner.

Leaders who have significant feelings of well-being, happiness, and peace in their lives are less distracted, and therefore best able to identify team success opportunities and help their teams perform at the highest levels. Opportunities usually come disguised as problems, complications, or setbacks. So as a leader, if your own life is chaotic, unfulfilling, pessimistic, or generally unhappy—you'll be much less inclined to recognize these as new opportunities and spend the personal energy to tackle them. You'll miss potential team success opportunities because they aren't wrapped with a red bow and an attached gift card that has your team's name on it. The good news is that you can learn to improve your personal well-being, and in doing so, improve your capacity to recognize success opportunities for your team.

My research into expanding one's opportunity awareness revealed that there is a major movement going on in the world of human behavior. This movement is called "positive psychology" and was started by Professor Martin Seligman at the University of Pennsylvania. His research proved that there is a direct link between someone's measureable well-being and their subsequent levels of happiness, health, and job performance. He also proved that we can learn to improve our well-being—and thus improve our health, happiness and job performance.

This positive psychology movement is in direct contrast to the teaching of "abnormal" psychology that has dominated the prior 40 years. Instead of trying to identify and fix "what's wrong" in someone, the positive psychology movement identifies "what's right" and provides a path to understand and improve on the strengths of an individual, with the goal of increasing well-being. The research is clear on this: we can each improve our well-being without psychotherapy, drugs, or other interventions. It seems that when "interventions" such as therapy cease, the abnormal behavior inevitably returns—however, Seligman proved that by increasing well-being (happiness), the abnormal behavior is drastically reduced or eventually eliminated, and can be self-controlled. Seligman's research has led to a worldwide movement to apply the learnings on well-being and happiness, beginning right with children in early education, and continuing throughout our lives—it's called the Authentic Happiness Movement!

In his book, *Authentic Happiness*, Seligman outlines three happiness pathways: "the Pleasant Life" is happiness in the Epicurean sense of savoring and appreciating life's pleasures; "the Engaged Life" is happiness found through achieving success by consciously using our highest talents and being "in the flow" as often as possible; and "the Meaningful Life" is happiness in belonging to or serving something larger than oneself. Seligman proposes that complete "Authentic Happiness" can be achieved by living a life that satisfies all three pathways to happiness—a state which he calls the "Full Life."

During my research for this book, I had the opportunity to hear Dr. Seligman speak at a professional conference—not having heard of him or the positive psychology movement before then. I was intrigued, and my subsequent investigation into Seligman's Authentic Happiness theory filled in many gaps I had in mind about how to develop a reliably repeatable methodology to create an unstoppable Surging Team. The ingredient that finally made the BOLD Success Principle reliably repeatable was, in fact, when I recognized that I had to incorporate Seligman's scientifically proven concept into our program. Once a leader accepts the responsibility for, and works to increase his personal happiness and well-being, he sets himself on a path to dramatically increase his awareness of team success opportunities. He can then help his team increase their individual happiness, well-being, productivity and even their health.

In his books, *Authentic Happiness* and *Flourish*, Dr. Seligman identifies five characteristics of well-being and happiness, which he synthesizes using the acronym PERMA. [1]

P = Positive Emotions. Positive emotions are the foundation of happiness. To improve your leadership skills, it is important to work to increase the positive emotions in your life. Identify people, activities, and things that give you pleasure and make time for them in your life to bring more positive emotions and enjoyment into your day.

E = Engagement. You can increase your engagement at work by minimizing distractions and improving concentration on the work at hand. This helps you slip into a "state of flow." The more often and longer you can stay in flow, the more productive and aware you'll be at work.

R = Relationships. Let go of relationships that are destructive, and embrace those that bring you happiness. Repair important but damaged relationships, as much as it's in your control to do so. Building a better and stronger relationship takes time and effort, so resolve to spend time with the important people in your life. If you don't, those relationships will atrophy and won't be there as strongly as they could be when you need them.

M = Meaning and Purpose. Everyone needs a Personal BOLD Purpose, something higher than their own needs and desires, to bring meaning to their lives. Being a great Mom or Dad, volunteering for a worthy charity, or participating in volunteer activities are all BOLD Purposes you can choose for your life. Reflect on what most connects you with others, and make time for these activities and roles. At work, if your team has a shared understanding and commitment to a BOLD Purpose, they will collectively and individually perform better.

A = Accomplishment. Be sure to spend time on personal improvements that you want to accomplish in your life. Finishing a college program or being a contributing member of a successful team are accomplishments that will bring you satisfaction and happiness.

Seligman's research positively correlates high PERMA scores with greater well-being, productivity and health. I believe that the reason high PERMA scores result in increased productivity is because they also signal an increased capacity to be aware of success opportunities.

So how do you start to increase your well-being, using the above PERMA model? Seligman recommends that you begin by becoming aware of our own character strengths, the positive traits that make you uniquely who you are. Once you know your character strengths, you can use your top five highly developed strengths, which he calls your "signature strengths," more often—and increase your happiness by doing so. Seligman proved that if you consciously use your signature character strengths more often, your PERMA scores improve *in all areas of your life.* [2]

What are your possible character strengths? Seligman believes there are 24 of them, which he groups into six major categories:

1. *Wisdom and knowledge.* Strengths that involve the acquisition and use of knowledge: Curiosity, Love of learning, Judgment, Ingenuity or Creativity, Social Intelligence, and Perspective
2. *Courage.* Strengths that allow one to accomplish goals in the face of opposition: Bravery, Perseverance, and Honesty or Integrity
3. *Humanity.* Strengths of tending to and befriending others: Love and Kindness
4. *Justice.* Strengths that build healthy community: Teamwork, Citizenship, Fairness, and Leadership
5. *Temperance.* Strengths that protect against excess: Humility, Prudence, and Self-Control
6. *Transcendence.* Strengths that forge connections to the larger universe and provide meaning: Appreciation of Beauty and Excellence, Gratitude, Hope, Humor, Spirituality, Forgiveness, and Zest

After examining this list, how well do you know yourself and your own signature character strengths? If you want to find out, take the VIA Survey of Character Strengths, a relatively short questionnaire developed by Dr. Seligman, available on his website at www.authentichappiness.org. It's a free character strength assessment that takes about 15 minutes to complete. Once you take this survey of character strengths, you'll receive your personal strength ranking on all 24 character traits, and, most importantly, you'll find out your top five signature character strengths. You can also find a link to the VIA survey on our website, BOLDbreak.com.

SIGNATURE CHARACTER STRENGTHS

If you went off just now and took this test, did you guess your signature character strengths, or did any surprise you? Whatever they were, do not worry or try to make comparisons with other people. There is no best arrangement of your character strengths; there's just a unique arrangement for each person. All 24 character traits are useful, regardless of their ranking, and the five highest strengths that you find most natural to you are your "signature strengths." These are your most highly developed strengths, and you should rely on them to solve vexing problems. Now is a good time to get to know yourself better, and appreciate your signature character strengths. Indeed, Dr. Seligman recommends that in order to achieve more success and more happiness in performing your work, you should find ways to use your signature strengths more often when solving problems.

Improving yourself and your team

Regardless of your current, perceived level of self-actualization, all of us can benefit from continued efforts to improve ourselves and increase our personal happiness. It's critical for team leaders and company owners to understand themselves as well as possible. Identifying and consciously applying and using your signature strengths to solve problems will improve your personal well-being and your work performance. Using your newly discovered signature strengths will increase your level of engagement at work, increase your ability to recognize opportunities, and allow you to more effectively lead your team to success.

After a team leader helps herself, she can then help her team members raise their PERMA scores by helping them become aware of and use their own signature strengths more often at work—consciously affirming those strengths when her team members display them. Becoming aware of and encouraging the use of the signature strengths that each of your team members already possesses is critical to their individual happiness and well-being. Raising everyone's PERMA score is a milestone on the critical path to developing an unstoppable Surging Team.

If you have people in your company in team leadership positions who have unhappy and chaotic lives, and who are unwilling to work on improving their own well-being, personal happiness and peace, you should consider finding ways to remove them from their leadership positions. You cannot let them lead, as they will be ineffective in recognizing team success opportunities or developing their team's success potential.

If you are a leader, train yourself to look differently at the challenges you and your team face in achieving success. Both entrepreneurs and intrapreneurs are responsible for driving teams that are challenged to accomplish difficult and elusive objectives. As you will learn, team success intersects every one of the PERMA components: positive emotions, engagement, relationships, meaning, and accomplishment. The more you exercise your own signature strength awareness, and then encourage your team to recognize and engage their signature strengths—the happier and more productive your team will become. They'll be able to sustain longer periods of engagement at work, as well as use their signature strengths to overcome daunting obstacles.

So dedicate yourself to improving your own happiness and well-being. Prepare your heart and mind to be open to learning more than you'd ever imagined about your business, about the people you need to lead, and especially about yourself. This knowledge will go a long way toward enhancing your ability to recognize team success opportunities—and seize them for your team. The more opportunities your team has to develop their team success potential, the sooner they will become an unstoppable Surging Team.

Increase your well-being by re-establishing peace and trust with your critical inner circle

Relationships are one of the 5 PERMA components, and a major source of your happiness—or your sadness. As much as it's in your ability to do so, every team leader benefits from working to repair any damaged personal relationships with a spouse, children, and with their critical inner circle of friends. As an entrepreneur or corporate team leader, you'll need the support of your spouse and your critical inner circle of family and friends more than you may realize.

Work each day to affirm, or if necessary, re-establish peace and trust with your critical inner circle. You may be asking a few of them to participate in your entrepreneurial endeavor in a critical advisory capacity for you. Take this seriously, as you'll need the people who love you to trust that you value their input. Listen to their advice, especially when you ask for it. If you don't take their advice seriously, they'll know it, and they won't trust you the next time you ask.

BOLD Success is multi-faceted and more than just financial

What good is it to gain financial success and yet lose your most important relationships? Surround yourself with people who support you and let go of relationships that pull you back. You may not be able to hold on to all your relationships. Some people are spiraling in a cycle of unhappiness and defeat, and they may refuse to embrace a functionally positive relationship with you. They can't help you and they don't want your help either. If you're able, you may have to let them go, or at least deemphasize their input and importance in your life.

THE NIGHT I LET MY WIFE SAVE OUR BUSINESS

My wife and I were in very different places after I left my corporate job and started my franchise business. I'd simply been away too much, and she had no visibility into that major part of my life. Six months into starting my franchise business, I sat at the kitchen table trying to think. I was worried beyond belief. I'd used all my start-up capital to start my franchise business, and I was now staring at significant net losses *each month*. It was late at night, and I'd set aside my all-too-real fear of financial ruin so I could focus on assembling a "last chance" marketing campaign. That's when my wife came in to check on me.

"Scott, what are you working on now? It's late. Why don't you come to bed?"

I looked up from my pile of envelopes and letters to see my wife with concern on her face.

"I'm trying to send out some marketing letters to get some new clients for the business. This can't wait, so I'm just going to keep working tonight until I get this done."

This was a difficult time for us, and our marriage was not doing well. Although she suspected things with the business were not going great, I was afraid to share the extent of my worries with her.

On this night, my wife saw the mountain of letters and envelopes in front of me.

"You already worked all day, Scott. Can I help you do it?"

It would have been easy just to say "No, I'll take care of it," and continue on as the solitary loner who won't accept help. But on this night, maybe due to Divine intervention, I paused, and gave the response that set us on a new success trajectory, on multiple fronts.

"Yes, you can help. I can teach you how to help me do this."

This late night conversation turned out to be the start of a sustained and successful marketing effort, led by my wife, not me, which turned our business around. One fragile conversation between a humbled new business owner and his wonderful, concerned wife saved my business, and possibly our marriage.

Part of a successful leadership journey is to take the opportunity to build your career around a positive foundation. Entrepreneurial and intrapreneurial leadership offers you many opportunities to learn and grow. Consider forgiving anyone that failed or harmed you; do not let anger and resentment have power over you in your new endeavor. You don't have to seek them out, just forgive them in your heart, and move on.

What if you do feel angry and vengeful at someone? You have to learn to channel that anger . . . and then let it go. There are no perfect CEO's, employees, or opportunities. There's just you and a bunch of mostly average people, in various life situations, who on any given day will inevitably make some less than perfect decisions that may directly affect your business and cause you to become angry. When they do, don't let anger drive you to do unproductive things. Anger and revenge have been used throughout history as a powerful motivator to achieve astonishing victories—but they also cause unhappiness and poor health. You might be able to use your feelings of anger as an immediate source of energy, sort of like a secret weapon to help motivate you—but then let it go.

Developing team success potential

After becoming aware of an opportunity, the second component of mastering this first BOLDskill is for you, the team leader, to gather your courage, and *seize* the opportunity for your team. Just recognizing it isn't enough. You need to inspire and lead your team on a success adventure, overcoming the inevitable challenges and obstacles associated with the opportunity, while staying within budget and inside your stated time commitment.

"Team success potential" is the ability of the team to achieve success once an opportunity is identified and seized by the team leader. That is how the team learns to achieve difficult goals, overcome inevitable obstacles, and develop the feeling that they'll always win. A Surging Team develops an unstoppable success potential, and always finds a way to win. By engaging in multiple team opportunities, and achieving success, a team develops their potential for more. This makes them ready when a really important opportunity presents itself. "The harder you practice, the luckier you get!" as the saying goes.

How can you improve your ability to "gather your courage and seize opportunities" once those opportunities are identified? Previously I challenged you to become more aware of your own character strengths, the positive traits that make you uniquely who you are. I directed you to the "VIA Survey" link on our website, and encouraged you to take the VIA Survey of Character Strengths and receive your personal and unique strength ranking of the 24 character traits. One of those strengths is bravery.

But what if bravery is not one of your top strengths? Don't feel badly. Remember, there are 24 character strengths, and only the top five are considered your signature strengths. But we all have "a little of each" of the 24 strengths, and it turns out that you can learn to engage any of them when you need to by using one of your top five strengths.

For example, one of my signature strengths is persistence, so I call on this to help me take a brave action that allows me to succeed. Accountants and analytical people tend to have a high degree of "prudence" and are keenly aware of and avoid risks. Prudent people are needed in an organization, to balance the sometimes "too hopeful" views of optimists, like those in the marketing department! If you have a high degree of prudence, and prefer to thoroughly analyze each aspect of a big decision, then the first step for you is to realize that your inclination is to do just that. This can then be a way to call on your bravery.

Leverage your team's combined individual strengths

No matter where bravery falls in the ranking of your character strengths, take a careful look at the potential opportunity, and don't make an overly optimistic, pessimistic, or otherwise hasty decision. Look at the opportunity in light of your team's combined strengths. Consider what character strengths your team would need to exhibit if you take on this opportunity. Do you know each of your team members' signature strengths? Given their strengths, what is your estimation that your team will succeed? Consider if you are being overly pessimistic, or if you need to dial your "prudence" strength back just a little and look at the opportunity with more optimism, in light of knowing your team's combined signature strengths.

The good news for those leaders with prudence as a signature strength is that it hurts the team if their leader seizes an opportunity that they don't complete successfully—so rejecting overly risky opportunities is wise. However, if you are rejecting too many opportunities, it may be that you need to dial "down" your prudence while raising up another of your character strengths for some balance—such as your strength of curiosity, leadership, or creativity. Brainstorm with your team and get their feedback on an opportunity you're considering. Engaging your team in the evaluation of an opportunity is also a great way to increase their feeling of "ownership" in the eventual decision.

One exercise to evaluate an opportunity is to prepare a Strength Gap Analysis with your team. This exercise shows "where we are" on one side of the diagram, and "where the opportunity could take us" on the other side—and the gap in the middle is where you need to explore to "build a bridge using the team's combined character strengths" to succeed in the opportunity. The exercise helps you identify, for a given opportunity, what strengths will be needed. I have included the Signature Strengths Org Chart and the Surging Team Strength Gap Analysis in Appendices B and E of this book for you.

After identifying your team members' signature strengths, and completing a Strength Gap Analysis on what strengths are needed, you can make an informed decision on whether those strengths are present in enough capacity on your team and whether they can be leveraged to achieve the objective. It's OK to decline an opportunity, as long as you remember the BOLD Success Principle, and that you are not waiting for the *perfect* opportunity, just an *ordinary* one. You don't want to pass up too many opportunities, because a team that doesn't get to exercise their success potential will not be prepared when their leader finally engages them in a really important team success opportunity. Like a sports team, a work team must practice their success skills or they will atrophy and be woefully unprepared with the real game is on.

On the other hand, a leader who has bravery as their highest strength may need to use his other strengths to balance it out. Like a general in a battle, you have to take stock of the risks. What good is leading "Pickett's Charge" directly into overwhelming enemy fire? What team wouldn't be demoralized by a crushing defeat?

Learning to seize an ordinary opportunity

Once a leader identifies a team success opportunity and demonstrates the courage to engage his team and commit to achieving the objectives associated with the opportunity, the BOLD Success Principle requires the leader to not just take on the opportunity—but to *seize* it. Our language is precise here.

When we seize something, we don't let it go without a fight, and even in a fight, we still refuse to let it go. That is the attitude of commitment to complete the success opportunity that a team leader must have. Once his team is engaged and committed, the leader must assure that the team's objectives are met—because that's how the team's success potential is built. We live in a competitive economy, and that assures us of a contest. It is not only an economic contest, but also one of character and preparedness. This contest is played out both inside the team's own company, as well as in the marketplace. Our BOLDskills for Accelerated Team Success are designed to prepare the team leader for both arenas.

One caveat: The team leader who seizes an opportunity will inevitably be faced with multiple obstacles to achieving success. They come in the form of delays, misunderstandings, unscheduled time-off, human error, betrayal, loss of key staff, unforeseen events like weather and natural disasters, and even economic instability—the potential list of blockades is endless. How the leader responds in the face of these obstacles will determine whether the team adds to their team success potential and gains the momentum of an unstoppable Surging Team—or blames failure on a convenient antagonist, from a plentiful roster of suspects.

Fear is a significant factor in succumbing to these persistent and plentiful antagonists. As leaders, we must always perform a mental cost-benefit calculation of whether the gains of continuing to pursue a goal are worth the unexpected professional, personal and team costs. We must constantly think about questions like, "So what happens if we get behind schedule a few weeks? What if we need time to try out some options and alternatives before we go into real action? What impact will delays have on the team?" These questions matter, and must be able to be answered in the positive, because a Surging Team always achieves its objectives, on time, and within budget. An unstoppable Surging Team does not accept creeping defeatism.

Nobody wants to be seen as giving up or quitting. Seizing an opportunity puts your team in the spotlight and sets up increased scrutiny by your organization. It's easier and safer to "lay low," and not "volunteer" for more work—but that tactic defeats your main purpose of developing the success potential of the team you are leading. You want your team to feel unstoppable, and that once engaged "they'll always win." It takes practice to achieve this collective, positive spirit.

Here is an exercise for team leaders to use to identify and overcome fears—fears that keep the team leader from identifying an opportunity, as well as fears that entice a leader to accept a modified or "scaled-down" version of the originally accepted success objective. We call this exercise the "ABCDE Exercise for Identifying and Overcoming Fear." The idea is for the leader to:

- Become **A**ware when fear is present
- Identify what automatic **B**eliefs accompany this fear
- Imagine the **C**onsequences of the actions you may take because of this fear
- Learn to **D**ispute this fear with facts so you can imagine new outcomes
- Feel **E**nergized by your ability to "argue with yourself" and help you change your habitual beliefs that follow fears you have.

If you can change your habitual negative beliefs about a fear, then you can change your reaction to develop a more accurate view of that fear and be in a better position to deal with it. The goal is to become skilled at undoing your damaging personal fear habit, which causes you to avoid opportunities, by becoming skilled at generating alternative, more accurate beliefs about your fears. This should feel energizing and freeing to you, allowing you to choose to accept opportunities that you may otherwise have declined, and refusing to give in to fears that block your path to success. We have included a worksheet for the ABCDE Exercise for Identifying and Overcoming Fear in Appendix F.

How do you know if you've achieved mastery over BOLDskill 1?

If you as the team leader can humbly look at each day as a new challenge, delighting in more potential opportunities for you and your team to use your collective signature strengths, courageously identifying and seizing team success opportunities, and then leading your team of ordinary people past obstacles to achieve success—then you as the team leader have mastered the first BOLDskill.

BOLD takeaways

- **The BOLD Success Principle:** Success follows a predictable course. It's not the brightest who succeed, or those presented with a perfect opportunity. Success follows those who have been given ordinary opportunities—and who have the presence of mind and the courage to seize them.

- Ordinary daily challenges are actually disguised "team success opportunities." They are a chance for you as the team leader to engage your team and utilize their collective talents to accomplish a team victory over an obstacle, a challenge, or a goal. Each victory will build the happiness, well-being, and productivity of each team member, as they participate in the team accomplishment.

- "Opportunity awareness" is the awareness of the team leader to identify team success opportunities that he can use to engage his team, achieve team success, and thereby develop the team's success potential.

- Take the VIA survey of character strengths from our website at BOLDbreak.com or from the authentichappiness.org website to identify your signature strengths. Start using them more often to increase your well-being, happiness, productivity, and health. As the team leader, the more you use your signature character strengths, the happier and more productive you'll become. You'll also increase your capacity to recognize team success opportunities.

- After being aware of an opportunity, the second component of mastering this first BOLDskill is for you, the team leader, to gather your courage and *seize* the opportunity for your team. Just recognizing it isn't enough. You need to inspire and lead your team on a success adventure—overcoming the inevitable challenges and obstacles, while staying within budget and inside your stated time commitment.

- "Team success potential" is the ability of your team to achieve success once an opportunity is identified and seized by the team leader. A Surging Team always finds a way to win, by learning to achieve difficult goals and overcome inevitable obstacles. By engaging in multiple team success opportunities, and then assuring the successful completion of each, a Surging Team develops their unstoppable success potential.

NOTES

[1] *Flourish: A Visionary New Understanding of Happiness and Well-Being* and *Learned Optimism: How to Change Your Mind and Your Life,* both books by Martin E. P. Seligman, Ph.D.

[2] Peterson, C., & Park, N. (2009). Classifying and measuring strengths of character. In S. J. Lopez & C. R. Snyder (Eds.), *Oxford handbook of positive psychology,* 2nd edition (pp. 25-33). New York: Oxford University Press. www.viame.org; Peterson, C., & Seligman, M. E. P. (2004). Character strengths and virtues: A handbook and classification. New York: Oxford University Press and Washington, DC: American Psychological Association.

Always use a formal business plan and include your team in the process

By failing to prepare, you are preparing to fail.
— BENJAMIN FRANKLIN

"Why are you showing this to us?" asked my middle-aged service technician.

"Because I want you to understand what we're trying to achieve, how we're going to do it, and when we need to get it done," I explained.

After a pause, my team member said, "I've never worked for a company that showed me their business plan before, so I wasn't sure why you showed it to us."

"It's not just my plan, it's *our* plan," I clarified.

The critical role a formal business plan plays in developing a Surging Team

Formal, written business plans are a tool for owners and team leaders to communicate the company's BOLD purpose to its employees, clients, prospects, and investors. Where are we going? How are we going to get there? When do we need to arrive? They act like a clear roadmap so everyone knows: "Here is the route we will take to get from where we are today to where we want to be in the next year or two."

A formal business plan lays out the "evolutionary change strategy" of the company or the team—because a business plan is about growth. It answers the question: How will my company or team grow over the next year? When pursuing difficult goals and facing the daily obstacles, fears, and pressures associated with those goals, your formal business plan provides you with a source of peace and resolve, knowing that your team is acting based on a well-thought-out plan.

Your business plan is also a strategic tool to communicate with others. Investors or lenders can use the information when forming a judgment about your company's ability to succeed. A formal plan says that you're serious about achieving your company's goals. Try to get a business loan without a formal business plan.

You'll also see how important a business plan is when you want to sell your business. We'll discuss this in greater detail when we get to BOLDskill 10 which is about laying the groundwork for the profitable, future sale of your business or division.

A formal business plan is also a way to direct and inspire your team members. Most workers have never seen a formal business plan, because privately-held companies tend to jealously guard their business plans (or don't have one to begin with). Even most publicly-held companies that make their business plan available to anyone are reluctant to proactively review their formal plans with their employees. Many companies don't see the value of providing strategic information to "low-level" employees who only need to act on their tactical job objectives.

The Surging Team recommendation is to use your formal business plan as a tool to inspire your team members around your company's overall strategy. I further recommend that you involve your employees in the process of creating your plan, so that it becomes a completely shared document. Involving the team members in the plan's development builds trust, and engenders a positive collective spirit among your team in a way that can't be quantified.

The entire team should feel accountable for achieving the goals contained in the plan—not just the team leader and company executives. To feel accountable, the team must feel they have an ownership stake—we call this "ownership engagement" or a "feeling of ownership." A team adopts ownership engagement by participating in the creation of the plan they'll be playing a part in, and then accepting the objectives as outlined in the plan as their own. In contrast, having an already-made plan imposed upon a team drives a wedge between "management" and "the ordinary people who have to get things done."

Many companies do not use a written business plan. Some of today's workers have gone decades in their careers without ever seeing a written business plan from their company. This top-down imposition of the company's plan and objectives no longer works in today's world, when companies must depend on their people to function as highly collaborative teams in order to effectively serve our large, service-based economy. In order to compete effectively in a marketplace where "customer satisfaction" and "service excellence" are key points of a company's brand distinction, you need team members who pursue their work objectives with the same passion as an owner, who feel ownership engagement. You need a team of people holding each other accountable to what they all agreed upon formally, each one being individually committed to do their part to achieve.

Don't listen to naysayers of business plans

From my experience, when business owners are asked why they don't have a formal business plan, some downplay its importance, while others even scoff at the idea. Some see it as a relic of a past management style, no longer relevant "in the new fast-paced econ-omy" we operate in where they claim long-range planning simply cannot be done. These "business plan debunkers" are sometimes very proud of their belief, and even embrace business-plan-de-bunking as a virtue. To them, it is hip to "reject over-planning, re-main fluid and flexible, and just wing it." Some of these debunkers like to tell a tale of some long-ago "back-of-the-napkin business plan" that still somehow "guides" their company today. Unfortu-nately, our memories are often imperfect rewriters of history.

When I owned my franchise business, many of my franchise owner peers did not operate from a written business plan each year. They had their reasons, but I was determined to succeed. I wanted to document and chart a course for success, and I wanted everyone working in my company to know that we were dead se-rious about our plans for growth. When I produced my 100-page business plan through team collaboration meetings, few of my peers understood why I bothered to take the time and involve my employees.

Entrepreneurs who are trying to increase the likelihood of suc-cess for their business or team need to reject the advice of such "back-of-the-napkin planners" and "business plan debunkers." As a leader, you need to use all the proven tools available to you, and to take the actions correlated with reliably repeatable business suc-cess. Unfolding old napkins kept in your wallet does not correlate with business success. Having a thoughtfully prepared, formal business plan is correlated with business success—just ask your banker.

The allure of "winging it" and "remaining fluid and flexible" can seem strong. But publishing a formal business plan, one that involved the participation of all company team members, is a Bold action that tells the world what your team intends to do—and dares anyone to try and stop them. It is also much more difficult for a company to randomly change course if they're operating from a formal business plan. A company that abandons its original strategy in favor of something that "seems more achievable," is a company that will fail to achieve any meaningful success. In a competitive economy, achieving above-average business results is difficult, far from comfortable, and requires the talent, commitment and resolve of the entire team to see the plan all the way through—and win.

Developing a formal business plan, and involving your team in its creation, is a component of achieving *reliably repeatable* business success. I have made it my second BOLDskill that a great team leader needs to master. There will always be other ways to achieve business success, but they may not be reliably repeatable. To reduce the risk of business or team failure, and increase your chances of success, you as the business leader need to use all the proven strategic tools you have—and a business plan is one of the best.

Be prepared to show your team's plan to anyone appropriate who asks—and show them how and when your company or team will achieve its objectives. Your business plan is your guide to whether you're on track to succeed, or if your team needs to adjust *now* in order to get back on track to achieving your objectives—on time and within budget.

Let's quickly summarize the benefits of a formal business plan. A formal business plan:

- Is a strategic tool to communicate your company's evolutionary change strategy
- Is a strategic tool to keep you focused on your company goals during times of stress
- Is a strategic tool to communicate to lenders and investors
- Is a strategic tool to show potential buyers when the time is right to initiate an acquisition discussion
- Increases the likelihood that your team will achieve its stated goals

- Increases the perceived value of your company
- Increases the "ownership engagement" of your team members because they had a part in creating it

Notice the frequent use of the word "strategic" in the above list of benefits. Your formal business plan is one of your most accessible strategic tools—helping all vested stakeholders understand why your company exists in the first place, and where it's headed.

THE ELEMENTS OF A GOOD BUSINESS PLAN

Below are the high level components of a business plan:

1. Executive Summary: An introduction to the company. Generally, the executive summary is written last, summarizing the salient points of the entire plan.
2. Company Description
3. BOLD Purpose / Mission / Vision
   a. BOLD purpose is the difference the company wants to make in the lives of their clients
   b. Mission is how the company will do it
   c. Vision is how the company envisions their products and services will impact the world
4. Product / Service Description
5. Industry Analysis: opportunities & threats
6. Marketing Plan
7. Competition: your company's strengths and weaknesses compared to competitors
8. Sales Strategy
9. Operations Plan
10. Management Team
11. Financial Plan: breakeven analysis, projected profitability, and ROI

How can I predict the future?

A key business plan section is the breakeven analysis. Business schools often teach students to use three breakeven projections:

- the best-case (optimistic)
- the worst-case (pessimistic)
- the "likely-case" projection (which can be an average of the other two)

My advice: NEVER use the optimistic projection when determining your budget needs and your target dates. I recommend that you use the likely-case or even the worst-case projection, as this will assure that your team has enough budget set aside to survive a worst-case scenario. It also sets your team up to meet, and if possible exceed, the objectives included in your plan. If the worst-case scenario is not acceptable, then use it as a benchmark and adopt slightly more optimistic objectives and timelines. But don't go full-on with the best-case scenario or you will unnecessarily set up your entire team for failure. As the team leader, you need to make sure your team always wins! They need to develop the feeling that they can't lose, that they are an unstoppable Surging Team.

How many inexperienced business leaders do you think use the above planning technique and err on the best-case side? I've seen far too many new business owners adopt the best-case scenario, and then run out of capital before achieving their objectives and begin the death spiral. How do you think team morale is when things start to spiral downwards?

The team leader needs to be a BOLD salesman for her team. Make sure your team has the opportunity to always meet or exceed the goals identified in the business plan. If you are a team leader inside a larger company, be sure to negotiate with other team leaders and anyone necessary to get the best terms for your team's goals in the company business plan. Try to build time and budget into your goal deliverables in order to allow you and your team time to "regroup" after encountering unforeseen success obstacles—and there will be plenty. You want your team to learn to believe that they will ALWAYS meet their objectives, on time and within budget—so they become an unstoppable Surging Team.

Setting up your team to fail to meet critical dates, or to run out of budgeted dollars, is teaching them that they will most likely not meet their objectives—that company goals are usually unrealistic and thus they can't be trusted. Your team needs to share the company's goals and believe that with the hard work of each team member, those objectives can be achieved.

What if your team is not directly involved in producing company revenues?

If your team isn't a profit center in a corporation, then you won't have a projected revenues section, but you should have measurable objectives to help other corporate divisions achieve their revenue goals. If you're not leading a key team that has the objective of helping your company or helping corporate profit centers succeed in their revenue objectives, then you may soon be out of a job. The first people a company lets go when the budget gets tight are those who are in "cost centers." So if you are leading a support team, then create and adopt a BOLD purpose that demonstrates a direct link to helping the true company "profit centers" achieve their objectives. Negotiate with the profit centers, ask their team leaders how your team can support them, and become a critical part of their planning. You want your peers to see you and your team as critical to *their* success.

Getting your team involved in planning

If possible, it is a great benefit to get your team involved in creating your team's business plan. If your company's business plan is usually created by the executive team, without your team's involvement, at least take the time to review the plan with your team. This is the start of a trusting leader/ member relationship, one where the entire team owns and is accountable to the company's plan and understands their role in the plan. Agree on how to measure progress on plan objectives that rely on your team. Use all the techniques at your disposal to get your team's buy-in to the business plan.

Even if your team is not directly included in the business planning process, you can use an off-site meeting with your team to review the company's business plan and your team's plan objectives. The off-site meeting will emphasize the importance of planning with them by removing your team members from their normal work environment. Your leadership objective is to achieve a sense of shared accountability for achieving the team's objectives as outlined or gleaned from the company's business plan, so be creative and try to engage multiple character strengths in your business plan review process in order to impart a strong sense of "ownership engagement" to your team members.

What about unforeseen obstacles that can affect your plan?

How can you possibly know *exactly* how and when you'll achieve something that will take months or years to achieve? This a good question, but there is an answer.

Rarely does a business plan go exactly as intended. It's not a document to be created, read, and then put in a binder and filed away. Your plan needs to be continuously referenced, evaluated, and updated. If you fall behind or face unforeseen obstacles, your team's tactics must be adjusted—using the creativity and innovative ideas of the entire team, with the single-minded goal of achieving ultimate success as outlined by your plan. Innovation emerges when urgency, accountability, and creative collaboration are present. All businesses and teams must adapt to the new dynamic business environment of today's world, one that demands constant adjustments to remain relevant and on target.

If you need to adjust your plan, be thoughtfully ruthless to get your team back on track to achieve the objectives. In order to maintain the integrity of your team's success potential, you may need to fire people who are dragging down the team. Accept no excuses for not meeting your plan objectives. If needed, negotiate better deals with clients, vendors, your team, and your peers. Stare down your fears of needing to be liked by everyone. If you feel you need to be liked, then go adopt a Golden Retriever from the nearest pet rescue center. Nobody wants to hang around a loser, but everyone wants to surround themselves with proven winners. If you run out of capital, or exhaust your division's budget, bad things start to happen, and it only gets worse from there. Lobby on your team's behalf and make certain your team always achieves their stated objectives.

We don't have the time to write a business plan!

Demonstrated skill at writing effective, formal business plans is required by most MBA programs. Why? Business schools correlate a well-written plan with higher business success rates. It's what serious business owners and leaders do. If you Google phrases like, "Why do businesses succeed?" or "Why do businesses fail?" you'll find that having or not having a formal business plan is a common theme in the search results.

I always enjoyed developing a formal business plan for the year ahead. During the planning process, the possibilities for my team seemed so endless. I recall it was a highly anticipated staff meeting when my team and I walked through our business plan draft together, at an off-site meeting, for the majority of several days. I intentionally made this a face-to-face review meeting in order to gauge my team's reactions to the plan draft and get their feedback before adding any final adjustments.

You need an edge to compete effectively, and a formal business plan is a critical component of that edge. At the minimum, if you are unable to spend the time developing a complete, formal business plan, then use a written *100–day action plan* to focus your team on their mutual objectives for the next 3 months. The key features of a 100–day business plan include the goals, deliverable dates, budget, how achievement will be measured, and who or which team members are specifically accountable. Here is a form you can use to create a 100–day business plan.

100-DAY BUSINESS PLAN

Objective/goal: Must be measurable in terms of output, sales, cost, time, team	
Ultimate accountability:	
How will goal achievement be measured?	
How does this goal align with your team's BOLD purpose?	
Expected results: Must be clear, controllable by your team, and realistic	
Budget available for this goal:	
Goal deliverable date:	
Action steps:	

BOLD takeaways

- The Surging Team depends on shared goals and a feeling of "ownership engagement" by all team members in achieving those goals. A business plan is your company's evolutionary change strategy, and outlines how you intend to get from where you are today, to where the company wants to be in the next year. A formal business plan is a strategic tool to communicate its goals and its BOLD purpose with anyone—either internally or externally, that the company needs to bring into alignment and support its drive to goal achievement.

- There will always be other ways to achieve business success, but they may not be reliably repeatable. To reduce the risk of business and team failure, and increase your chances of success, you as the team leader need to use all the proven tools you have—and a formal business plan is one of the best tools.

- If you find it difficult to draft a business plan for the entire year, then break it up and develop 100–day business plans. Put this 100–day plan in writing so you can review it each day, share it with your team, and make sure it's your top priority to take the actions needed each day to achieve your 100–day objectives.

- As the leader of your Surging Team, you need to assure that that your team always achieves its objectives—on time and within budget. If you thus need to adjust your plan, be thoughtfully ruthless to get your team back on track to achieve the original business plan objectives.

- If your team isn't directly involved in creating the company's business plan, be creative in finding ways to impart a feeling of ownership engagement in the plan's goals among your team members. Use an offsite meeting to review the plan with your team, and invite your team members to identify what their role is in the overall company plan.

- If your team is not a profit center for your company, then work with other corporate teams that are directly involved with driving revenues and ask them how your team can help in their success. Become a key part of their planning process.

Identify and Adopt a BOLD Purpose

Watch your thoughts: they become words;
Watch your words: they become actions;
Watch your actions: they become habits;
Watch your habits: they become your character;
Watch your character: it becomes your destiny.

— ATTRIBUTED TO VARIOUS AUTHORS

Companies use three different but related terms to describe the impact they want to make as a result of doing business.

- *Purpose* is the difference the company wants to make in the lives of people
- *Mission* is how the company will do it
- *Vision* is how the company envisions their products and services will impact the world

Of the three, *Purpose* is the most impactful for the employees of a company—and for your team. It hits us where we're most vulnerable—while we're interacting one-on-one with other people—and gives us the courage and voice to move beyond skepticism, fear, conflict, and uncertainty, when we can pursue our company's purpose in the marketplace.

In her book, *Selling with Noble Purpose,* Lisa McLeod insightfully writes about her research showing the significant, positive impact that a Noble Sales Purpose (NSP) has on a company's profitability. When a company successfully adopts and imparts an NSP to their employees—one they can personally identify with and internalize—the fortunes of that company tend to multiply. For salespeople especially, an NSP helps them feel empowered that their role is to "help" their clients, not just "sell stuff to them." But a company's NSP has to be a noble one in order to have this effect on individuals. There is something inside us all that intuitively understands when we're engaging with something beyond ourselves, something BOLD and worthy of our efforts and our allegiance.

For my intentions in this chapter, I use the term "BOLD purpose" to represent this same noble feeling and belief that McLeod talked about. Having a BOLD purpose helps the company and the team to believe they are impacting all people who come into contact with them in a significant, worthy, and meaningful way. In order to fully engage and be most productive in our work, we need to believe that everyone who hears our team's BOLD purpose—whether it be a team member, a client, a prospect, a vendor, or a peer—will see its sublime importance and its BOLDness.

It's not hard to imagine how our individual lives are improved when we live according to an internalized BOLD purpose. Consider the impact of many universally-acknowledged inspirational leaders, such as Abraham Lincoln and the sense of noble and BOLD purpose that he lived by. As you learned in the first BOLDskill discussion about PERMA and the five elements of well-being and happiness, the "M" in PERMA stands for Meaning. As humans, we're happier and experience higher levels of well-being when we have a sense that what we're doing has meaning that extends beyond ourselves.

This concept of a BOLD purpose is so powerful and important to our behavior, that I include it in the BOLDskills for Accelerated Team Success. BOLD purpose refers to the phenomenon of improved individual and company performance, when employees or team members identify with and internalize a company's belief in how it will positively impact the lives of everyone that comes into contact with their products, services, or the people working for them.

In order to increase individual well-being and happiness, we also encourage everyone to consider thoughtfully adopting a *personal* and a *professional* BOLD purpose for their own lives as well.

Adopting a personal BOLD purpose

"Great to meet you, Roger. What's your business?" I said, shaking hands with a stranger at a Chamber of Commerce networking event. I had been to a few of these in the past, and hadn't planned to attend this particular business opening ceremony, but here I was on my lunch hour, attempting to mingle.

"I'm a business vision consultant," said Roger.

"Interesting, how many clients do you have?" I asked, not sure what it was that he did.

Smiling broadly, Roger said, "Well, I think I'm about to get my newest client—YOU," he replied.

Roger was an older, grey-haired fellow, with a pastoral demeanor of wisdom. Having been in business for only three months, I wondered if I really needed advice like he could offer. But I felt isolated and increasingly fearful as I navigated my business start-up. I quickly assessed the opportunity of hiring him. I believe that the people we meet and the circumstance we find ourselves in do not happen by random chance. Our situations are the result of an inseparable combination of decisions and a BOLD purpose designed to arrange all things for good. But do we see the opportunity in such seemingly random interactions? I thought about it and decided maybe this guy was meant to help me.

"How much do you charge?" I asked tentatively.

We came to an agreement on his fee, and I hired Roger as my business vision consultant, still not quite sure what that was.

For the next six months, Roger and I met once a week to discuss my challenges. He gave me thoughtful homework, and we reviewed it each time we met. As we sifted through a variety of issues each week, one topic was a regular on my list: my marriage. It turned out that my major challenge was not the obvious business start-up problems, but rather it was my concern for my family, as my wife and I were having relational problems at the time. This portended danger for me on multiple fronts. Roger recognized it, and together we developed a "vision mantra," which I now recognize as a Personal BOLD purpose. He printed my Personal BOLD purpose on some business cards for me—so that I could carry it in my wallet and remember my resolve when things inevitably got tense at home. The business card read:

"My vision is to build a successful business
in the context of a healthy marriage."

I am very grateful to Roger. He helped me identify and embrace a personal BOLD purpose, one that helped me focus on rescuing my marriage during those uncertain early days of my business start-up. I still have the card with this vision mantra printed in now-faded black ink. I plan to keep it forever as a reminder of what was, and still is, most important in my life. It was a powerful message for me to see it written down and to own it.

I have had many occasions to share this personal story of Roger and his help with my marriage. Some people would inevitably approach me after I shared it and reveal their own struggles of relationship breakdown after they started their businesses. After hearing my story, more than one business owner has confided in me, "My wife said she's going to divorce me if I can't turn this business around. What can I do?"

As I discussed in the first BOLDskill, "positive Relationships" is the "R" in our PERMA model. It is a major component of our well-being, and hence, of our ability as team leaders to increase our opportunity awareness and to succeed in achieving our goals. A failing marriage, an unhappy relationship, or trouble in your family—these are all major obstacles to well-being, happiness and success for many people. Such stories are very sad and appear to be significantly correlated to underperformance by the affected person. They ultimately drain the team and hurt the company that depends on that leader's ability to consistently perform.

Leading a business is an all-consuming challenge. If your priorities are not clear from the beginning, you might let the unrelenting business pressures bearing down on you overshadow your personal relationships. To combat that, increase your odds for both personal and team success, and do whatever you need to do to appreciate the people you love, each day, so that relational breakdown doesn't debilitate you. I want you to succeed, so identifying your personal BOLD purpose and then adopting it, is a major component of your personal happiness and your success as a team leader.

Adopting a professional BOLD purpose

Just as a *personal* BOLD purpose can be a vital force of happiness and well-being in your life, it's also critical that your company identify and adopt a thoughtful and powerful *professional* BOLD purpose—one that inspires you and your team to achieve amazing things together. When your team faces a difficult business situation, and you've seemingly exhausted all your options to succeed, how will your team respond in that moment of doubt? If your team has embraced a BOLD purpose, one in which each team member is completely vested —then you have an edge that most companies and teams don't have.

If you're leading a corporate unit, your unit can adopt its own BOLD purpose, as long as it fits within your company's overall mission. You've been given the authority to lead a team using the company's most valuable resources in order to achieve success in attaining its corporate objectives, and you'll need your team to share your commitment and passion to achieve these objectives. A shared BOLD purpose assures your team will be pulling together. Your team's BOLD purpose is the reason everyone would rather work without sleep—than to miss an important client deadline.

If you're leading a support team, a team not directly related to the sales process, then consider adopting a BOLD purpose for your team that demonstrates a direct link to helping the company "profit centers" achieve their objectives. Negotiate with the profit centers, ask their team leaders how your team can support them, and become a critical part of their planning. You want to position your team as supporting the most critical departments and functions of the company, and your BOLD purpose can help to do that.

Your team's professional BOLD purpose likely won't be revealed quickly or by accident. To identify it, you'll like have to conduct a sustained and focused effort. Be sure to take the time to make your purpose a meaningful statement. It should be powerful enough to be that "competitive marketplace advantage" of which Jack Welch, the legendary CEO of GE, talked about when he famously said, "If you don't have a competitive advantage, then don't compete." There will be some days, weeks, months, and even years in your career that you'll be hanging onto your team's BOLD purpose as your only lifeline to keep going. If your team's BOLD purpose isn't compelling now as you close your eyes and briefly meditate on it, then it will not motivate and inspire innovative behavior when your team really needs it.

Here are some ideas adapted from Lisa McLeod's book, *Selling with Noble Purpose,* to help you identify your company's or team's BOLD purpose:

1. Ask each team member to write a story about when they've been most excited about their work.

2. Discuss these stories and look for themes that hint at a possible BOLD purpose.

3. Think about how you can phrase your BOLD purpose statement. It should be:
   - short
   - easy to understand
   - exciting
   - make you proud to be part of it
   - positively impact people

4. Create several options for your BOLD purpose and let team members use them for a few days.

5. After trying them out, choose the one that most resonates with everyone as your team's BOLD purpose.

6. Once a BOLD purpose is identified and adopted, make sure you repeat it to yourself and your team at every opportunity, so that it becomes ingrained in their psyche.

An effective way to transmit your BOLD purpose throughout your company is to recite your team's success stories collected during this exercise and going forward that embody the team's BOLD purpose. Seek out new inspiring stories that can serve as new anecdotes to highlight your team's BOLD purpose in action. Then use such stories to demonstrate your BOLD purpose in action to others. Remind your team at every gathering you have about the times your team's BOLD purpose was behind a success that helped a client or colleague. Make these success stories part of the history and DNA of your team and part of each new team member's heritage. Create your own team legends and retell them every chance you get.

Your company's BOLD purpose—and the team self-talk and anecdotal stories that exemplify it—are critical to developing your team's unwavering belief in their ability to solve any problem that they encounter on their way to achieving unstoppable success.

Here's an example. In 2008, my franchise business was growing, but I had not identified a BOLD purpose for my company. That changed shortly after I hired a new senior computer technician, whom I will call Joe. This fellow seemed to be just a regular guy, but he also happened to be a U.S. Army Special Forces veteran. I suspected he didn't give up easily when I hired him.

One night around midnight, I had to call Joe about a client problem we were having.

"Joe, Client X's computer servers are still down, they've been down since late afternoon. I know you just drove 10 hours today, but is there any way you can help this client . . . tonight?"

I was aware that Joe's day had already started with his driving 5 hours, one way, to install a computer server at another client's main office in the state capital. He completed the work and then turned around and drove another 5 hours back the same day, getting home to his family after 10 p.m. That same afternoon though, a "game changing" client of ours had a computer failure, and by midnight their computers had already been down for several hours. A junior technician had tried valiantly all day to resolve the problem, but was unsuccessful. A few minutes before midnight, the junior technician called me to say he was mentally drained and out of ideas. I hated to do it, but I had to call and wake up Joe. There just wasn't any other option.

Amazingly, Joe answered his cell phone. After explaining the situation, he calmly replied, "Well, I'm not dead yet, so let's do it." Joe's answer humbled me. We met onsite at our client's office at

1:00 a.m. and began trying to restore their computing environment. By 6:00 a.m. we looked at each other and vocalized our dilemma, "We've got two hours left before the owner gets here." Then Joe, who had now worked six hours past midnight said, "I've got one more idea . . . let's give it one more try."

It was that last attempt that worked. When the owner walked in the door at 8:00 a.m. and asked us how it was going, we told him with pride that he was "up and running." Visibly relieved and appreciative, he thanked us. We knew that we'd solidified his trust. His confidence in our ability and in our absolute determination to get his computer system working was etched in stone. We gained a long-term client for life that night and created our own legend.

This story is what became the event that fueled our company's BOLD purpose: "We'll never give up if your computers are down."

Over the next few years, we repeated the story to ourselves, to new clients, to our friends and family. It gave my new employees an immediate and practical example of our BOLD purpose. It always put a swagger in our voices and lifted our countenance to tell that story. The legend gave our entire team the irrational confidence that we would eventually persevere, even when it seemed impossible. We simply refused to give up if our client's computer system was down. Each team member used it to guide their actions every day—even when nobody was watching them.

Knowing our BOLD purpose helped my team win again and again as our company grew. Even when we brought on new clients, were faced with new problems, outgrew our procedures, lost employees, hired new staff, and battled every day to overcome the myriad obstacles that a growing company faces—we still believed we'd win because we simply would never give up. Our BOLD purpose was the fabric that held us together throughout our tumultuous "start-up phase," and propelled my company to eventually win the "Franchise of the Year" and "Million Dollar Club" awards, on the way to achieving financial success.

What does it feel like to work for a company without a BOLD purpose?

"Do you have any questions for us?" the director of operations asked me.

"Yes, what is your company's mission?" I asked.

"Well, that keeps changing," the director chuckled, "and I can't remember what it is right now."

I was offered a job with the above company, but I didn't take it. Even without knowing the salary, the hours, the location, or anything else about the company, do you know why I could not take that job?

I could tell this company was not a place I'd flourish, because they had no BOLD purpose.

If you want to attract the best talent to work as team members, you need an impactful BOLD purpose, one that job applicants can imagine spending their valuable time, talent and energy pursuing. Without a BOLD purpose, your team is like a warship with a damaged rudder, wandering around a vast ocean, with a crew that's not sure where they're going or why, and certainly not passionate about it. In fact, most of them are just waiting for an opportunity to jump ship.

Your team needs an edge they can hold onto throughout all the challenges they'll face in their drive for success. A BOLD purpose gives them that edge, and helps everyone get right back up into the arena every time competitors, clients, detractors, or even colleagues knock them down. The most powerful of motivators for a team is to adopt and have a common commitment to a compelling BOLD purpose.

BOLD takeaways

- Your company's BOLD purpose is the difference the company wants to make in the lives of people that come into contact with it through its employees, products, and services.

- PERMA represents the elements of well-being and happiness in Seligman's theory of happiness. The "M" in PERMA stands for Meaning. We're happier and we experience higher levels of well-being when we have a sense that what we're doing has meaning that extends beyond ourselves. That is what a company's BOLD purpose provides.

- The "R" in PERMA stands for "positive Relationships." We encourage you to adopt a personal BOLD purpose, one that strengthens your most important relationships. Higher levels of well-being by the team leader are associated with increased team opportunity awareness. When the leader is happier, the team is happier and performs better.

- A BOLD purpose is a critical component of a Surging Team, and is the reason your team is willing to work, sometimes without sleep, than miss an important client deadline. It provides a powerful competitive advantage for your company.

- A Surging Team, empowered by their BOLD purpose, finds innovative ways around all obstacles in order to achieve success—refusing to give up. The competition can't defend against the indomitable spirit of a Surging Team and its innovative responses to opposition. Nobody sees them coming.

- Team self-talk and anecdotal stories that exemplify your professional BOLD purpose are critical in transmitting the Surging Team's indomitable spirit to all its members. New team members immediately become impacted by these stories, which become part of their automatic team heritage—just by joining the team.

BOLDskill 4

Provide ownership engagement, inspired leadership, and trusted management

The secret to change is to focus all of your energy
not on fighting the old, but on building the new.
— SOCRATES

When I ran my franchise business, our off-site owner peer-group meetings were a much anticipated and welcome quarterly event. The first night's dinner was the official kickoff to several days of meetings, but tonight there was an empty chair at the table.

"Why isn't John coming to our group meeting?" I asked the dean of our business owners' group.

"John's going out of business," he replied.

"What! Last month he was excited about his highest sales numbers ever. What happened?"

"He had a senior staff member quit a few months ago, and the fellow took half his client base with him. It was a huge loss and John is completely discouraged. He said his wife demanded he 'cut his losses' and find a corporate job."

After I heard that story about my peer's business failure, the lesson I learned impacted me, and it resonated so strongly that I have made it another of the BOLDskills.

Formulating the three natural group governance roles

As the company owner or team leader, you must *intentionally* guide the development of the natural group governance roles on your team, making certain that you accomplish these three goals:

- *Ownership engagement.* You must transmit a sense of ownership to your team.
- *Inspired leadership.* You need to motivate your team members.
- *Trusted management.* As the leader, you must ensure that you earn the trust and respect of each team member.

If you abdicate the intentional development of any of these three natural group roles or provide them *timidly* or in a *spiritless* way—you will suffer negative consequences in your team and your business.

Humans are social creatures, and we are most productive when we're in groups of other people striving together to achieve common goals. Every cohesive group will naturally develop three group governance roles: *ownership, leadership and management.* Team members need to know these roles are in place, in order for them to function as a cohesive group. If we, as team leaders, understand this and act intentionally to perform those roles, we will achieve sustained levels of "flow" and higher engagement in our team's work. It is the responsibility of the owner or the team leader to consciously and systematically provide these three critical group governance roles to all team members. When any of these roles are lacking, someone in the group will inevitably attempt to fill the void, or the group will begin to weaken and drift away from the efficient pursuit of its goals, sliding toward entropy.

BOLDSKILLS METHODOLOGY FOR INTENTIONAL DEVELOPMENT OF GROUP GOVERNANCE ROLES

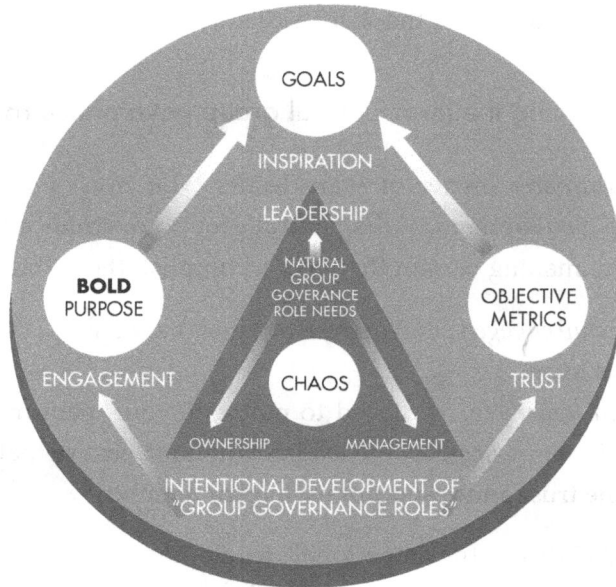

GOALS

INSPIRATION

LEADERSHIP

BOLD
PURPOSE

NATURAL
GROUP
GOVERANCE
ROLE NEEDS

OBJECTIVE
METRICS

ENGAGEMENT

CHAOS

TRUST

OWNERSHIP   MANAGEMENT

INTENTIONAL DEVELOPMENT OF
"GROUP GOVERNANCE ROLES"

What happens if entrepreneurs abdicate their group governance roles?

As a business owner, it's tempting to dream of delegating the difficult or uncomfortable group governance roles you don't personally want to perform in your business. You might think to yourself, "Why not hire someone to do the tasks I dislike?" Many business owners justify doing just that so they can focus on the tasks they'd prefer to work on. After all, your senior team members are likely the ones actually performing the technical or service work, and you did hire them, so why not just let them handle the leadership and management needs of the team too, whenever it seems convenient to do so?

Ah, but there's the rub. If you give in to this temptation, and abdicate or delegate the development of these group governance roles too early—before your company is viable enough to hire professional management—you will lose control of your leadership position, your company culture, and your company's direction.

Your employees will improvise, and the bold ones may start to believe that they are responsible for developing your company's culture and performing your team's critical group governance roles—not you. Worse, your clients may begin to agree with them.

I've seen this abdication of group governance role development repeated many times. It's what happened to my former colleague, John. He left a group governance role void, his senior team member filled it, and some of his clients followed. The team member who takes the initiative and becomes responsible for developing the group governance roles will soon threaten your influence on the team and with your clients. The group governance roles will develop and move forward without your guidance—because every cohesive group seeks them. However, if you *consciously* and *intentionally* manage them, you will be on your way to solidifying your leadership, and guiding your team toward achieving its goals.

What happens if intrapreneurs abdicate their group governance roles?

If you're responsible for leading a team inside a larger company, especially a team that's expected to creatively achieve their goals, then in addition to bringing knowledge and skills from your area of expertise, you were brought in to fill one or more of these critical group governance roles—even though it may have been unstated when you took the team leadership position. The problem is, when a company promotes a successful senior engineer or professional into a leadership role, the person often doesn't have the group leadership skills or even an awareness of their responsibility for the team's need to feel ownership engagement, inspired leadership, or trust in their management.

In many companies, senior engineers are often promoted into team leadership roles because it's believed that "being experts themselves makes them uniquely qualified to manage a team of experts." Because of this perception, these senior engineers are often not provided management/leadership training soon enough, or they don't take this training seriously—until things start going very badly on the team. A team with a leader who is not aware of, does not appreciate, or does not fully understand her role in guiding the intentional development of these group governance roles, will begin to drift or fracture—inevitably failing to achieve their objectives. Being trained as a software engineer, I've seen the phenomenon of promoting an unprepared senior technician into a team leadership role many times. These can be painful career experiences for all involved.

But I don't like performing those group governance roles!

As discussed in BOLDskill 1, I recommend that as the team leader, you can and must use your most highly developed signature character strengths to tackle difficult tasks, even if they are disagreeable to you. Tapping into your signature strengths when performing your group governance roles will improve your happiness and your success. (If you have not taken it, be sure to fill out the VIA Character Strength Survey to find your "signature character strengths.")

As the team leader, try performing the first of these three group governance roles—imparting a feeling of ownership engagement among your team members—by using your signature character strengths as your methodology to learn how to do it. Do this, even if your skill at it is imperfect, and even if you're not fond of it. Just choose one signature strength and use it to help you impart of feeling of ownership engagement to your team members. See the Worksheet below for an example.

Worksheet: Exploring how to use your signature strengths to accomplish BOLD skill 4

Let's say you choose "creativity" as your signature strength. Here are some ways how you apply this strength to accomplish one of the three group governance roles of BOLDskill 4.

You can use the "Worksheet for Exploring Additional Creative Uses of Signature Strengths," included in Appendix H, to get some ideas for how to use each of the 24 strengths to solve a problem or implement one of the group governance roles.

IMPARTING A FEELING OF OWNERSHIP ENGAGEMENT TO YOUR TEAM MEMBERS

Signature Strength	Creativity
Idea 1	Hold a contest on your team and solicit your team members' best ideas for what would make them feel like company owners.
Idea 2	Solicit your team members for their best stories about how your team's BOLD purpose made a difference in someone's life.
Idea 3	Begin to involve your team members in a monthly goal review process, and get their ideas on how to stay on track.
Idea 4	Consider suspending pay raises and instead institute a bonus plan if goals are achieved.

Now here's the same exercise with the next group governance role:

PROVIDING INSPIRED LEADERSHIP TO YOUR TEAM MEMBERS

Signature Strength	Creativity
Idea 1	Organize a volunteer community effort that your team members can participate in and support.
Idea 2	Invite an influential and inspiring public speaker to make a presentation to your team.
Idea 3	Ask your team for their ideas on how to put the company's BOLD purpose into action. Then implement one of those ideas.
Idea 4	Invite another team leader from your company to make a presentation to your team which explains what your team does for the company.

Now here's the same exercise for the last group governance role:

OFFER TRUSTED MANAGEMENT
TO YOUR TEAM MEMBERS

Signature Strength	Creativity
Idea 1	Identify some training opportunities for your team in the subject matter that is most closely related to their work.
Idea 2	Have each team member take the VIA survey of character strengths, and then create an org chart showing each member's signature strengths.
Idea 3	At your next meeting, ask your team members to identify instances where a signature character strength of one of the team members was on display.
Idea 4	Work with each team member to show them how they can use their signature strengths to accomplish each of their individual goals and objectives.

What happens if you don't intentionally transmit "ownership engagement?"

Your team's BOLD purpose is their bridge to engage with and feel ownership in the company's mission. Most team members have no financial ownership stake in the company, but all members of a Surging Team must feel that they have an ownership stake in the company's mission. A strong mutual feeling of ownership engagement in the group's mission, through its BOLD purpose, is imperative in order to intentionally evolve into an unstoppable Surging Team—a team whose members act like vested owners who refuse to give up.

Engagement is the second component of Seligman's 5 PERMA elements of well-being and happiness. Team members who are given an opportunity to engage with and feel ownership of their team's mission have higher well-being, are happier, and are more productive. Sounds like a Surging Team is developing!

Here's what happens if you, as the team leader or company owner, fail to intentionally transmit the feeling of ownership engagement with the team's BOLD purpose:

Your efforts to have your team adopt your company's BOLD purpose will fail, and you will lose a key tool for helping drive increased team performance. When an important goal is behind schedule, you may find that you're the only one who cares or tries to get it back on track. Owners are the last ones to quit, and you need a team that feels like "engaged owners" to assure that you're not standing alone one day. If you leave a void:

- Your team members may resent being treated like non-owners of the company's goals and find "creative" ways to replace their natural need to feel ownership engagement in the group. What they improvise to fill the void may be at odds with the team's or company's mission. For example, some key team members may become disgruntled and solicit others in the group to join them in a chorus of complaining.

- Your team members will be more susceptible to taking a job on another team, or at another company, where they believe they *will be* treated like owners.

- Without a strong feeling of "ownership engagement," feelings of happiness, well-being, health, and productivity begin to decline.

The longer you leave an "ownership engagement void," the more difficult it will be to close the gap. If you undertake an ownership engagement effort after too much time has passed, your employees may resist your intrusions into their alternate engagement behaviors—the ones they constructed in the absence of your intentional development. They may act out on these feelings of resentment—potentially sabotaging your effort and even your company. I've seen cases where the owner allows company culture and group role governance to evolve without conscious guidance, and then tries to come in and correct it later, only to get a big surprise. It's much easier to work consciously right from the start to transmit ownership engagement, and craft opportunities for each member to engage in the company's BOLD purpose and own it for themselves. Trying to intervene too late, after an informal alternate ownership engagement pattern has evolved among team members, is an unnecessary distraction and major risk factor.

What happens if you leave an inspired leadership void?

"Men, all this stuff you've heard about America not wanting to fight, wanting to stay out of the war, is a lot of horse dung. Americans traditionally love to fight. All real Americans love the sting of battle. When you were kids, you all admired the champion marble shooter, the fastest runner, big league ball players, the toughest boxers. Americans love a winner and will not tolerate a loser. Americans play to win all the time. I wouldn't give a hoot in hell for a man who lost and laughed . . . the very thought of losing is hateful to Americans."

—*Gen. George Patton, from the 1970 movie* Patton

In a war, tepid and uninspired leadership will get you and your team killed. Fortunately, you're not fighting a battle and risking your life or that of your team members. We have our brave military men and women to do that terrible and noble job. But your team of ordinary people still needs to be inspired to do difficult and extraordinary things in performing their work.

To accomplish the really hard jobs, leaders need to be out front, inspiring their team to win, providing BOLD goals, knocking down barriers, and then waving their team past the obstacles and on to success. I recommend that you regularly schedule time to talk to your full team, with a stated goal of discussing examples of inspirational behavior. In these meetings, identify something great that happened recently on your team or in your company. Ask your team members to identify inspiring situations to share with the group. Give them something they can think about until the next meeting. Your team members will respect you for working on your responsibility to provide inspirational leadership, and they will follow you as you lead them to achieving their objectives and becoming an unstoppable Surging Team.

I kept a personal journal during the years when I owned my IT franchise business. Let me share with you one of the inspirations I tried to give my team to let them know how important service quality and professional persistence was to our clients and to me:

"Team, consider carefully the challenge. We get discouraged, but we NEVER quit. This team has solved every service issue we've ever faced—and we're proud of that. We get tired, frustrated, and pushed to the edge of our abilities and energy—but each time, we gather ourselves again and renew the battle, until we succeed. Our clients hire us to remove their service worries, frustrations, and doubts. They need to know that we will never give up until we achieve this goal. We must win our clients' trust or we will lose their business—and we abhor losing. All of us are in the midst of determining whether we grow—or whether we fall back and regroup. We've come too far and have too much talent, ability, and indomitable spirit to quit. I won't choose the fallback path unless I'm forced to do so. I WILL NOT QUIT and YOU MUST NOT QUIT! If any one of you feels that they are not up to the challenge, then I ask you now for your resignation. We choose to fight until we either overcome our fears, our personal barriers, and our professional competition—or we are forced to retreat. Sleep on this challenge. Don't make a hasty decision. Consider it carefully. If you

choose to stay, I will challenge you beyond your current comfort zone. We will push ourselves and we will set our sights on achieving growth and success. If we do have to fall back, if we do have to relent, we'll do so knowing that we gave every ounce of our talent and our energy. We'll hold our heads high, and gather ourselves once again—and rejoin the fight. But, today we are not relenting! So consider this challenge carefully. I look forward to our staff meeting this Friday to discuss your thoughts around this decision."

Here's what happens if you leave an inspired leadership void on your team:

- Teams without inspired leadership regularly halt at obstacles—while the team leader either remains unaware of the barrier, accepts the delay and makes excuses for them, or abandons the objective. These teams have a low success potential; they do not feel unstoppable and they regularly fail to achieve their goals.

- Teams with uninspired leadership become fearful and combative when deadlines are mentioned. Turnover on the team becomes a problem, because nobody willingly wants to work on a losing team with an uninspiring leader.

- Someone on the team will step in and attempt to provide leadership, and if it's not the appointed team leader, then there will soon be management chaos.

- Your clients will notice who is providing the inspired leadership they need from your company. If it isn't coming from the appointed team leader, then you are in danger of losing your clients to anyone on your team who steps in to fill this void. This is the number one way that an established small business quickly goes out of business—loss of clients to a former team member.

- Uninspired leadership is not correlated with high team productivity. Your team will simply not be high performers, and will not evolve into an unstoppable Surging Team.

What happens if you leave a trusted management void?

A manager achieves "trusted" status when she identifies and relies on objective metrics to measure success toward achieving team and individual objectives. She is the chief administrator of company policies, including performance reviews and quality control. Arbitrary managers often use subjective measures to evaluate team member performance and team goal achievement. Effective and fair measurement of goal progress is critical to success. Everyone on the team, even those who are failing in their own objectives, respects and trusts a manager who consistently applies a fair metric for measuring their performance and goal attainment.

The biggest quality movement in the history of the industrialized world began with objectively measuring results, then taking actions to improve the results, and then measuring again, and again, and again. Dr. W. Edwards Deming brought his "quality improvement" research and techniques to the U.S. automobile industry, and both the major companies and the labor unions completely rejected his ideas. He then took his quality improvement ideas to Japan, which proceeded to use his simple ideas of objectively and regularly measuring product quality. As we all know now, Japan then proceeded to replace the United States as the world leader in automobile sales and quality—in less than a decade. That's what happens when management insists on remaining arbitrary and accepting subjective measurements. In the case of the auto industry, another country stepped in to fill the void.

As a manager, it's your responsibility to assure that your company and team members have a few clear metrics that are used to regularly and objectively measure progress toward achieving team and individual objectives. It's important that your team understands these metrics, has a hand in choosing them if possible, and knows the results of frequent metric measurements so they have an opportunity to adjust their work if measurements show they are off course. This is critical to keeping everyone informed of the team's current status, and on track in their individual quests for success. It is even more effective if you publish results of your measurements to the entire team or even the entire company. Nobody wants to be associated with underperformance or low quality work, and if everyone knows their efforts are being measured, monitored and even published, they tend to perform better. That's known as the Hawthorne Effect, and it's been in use by quality assurance teams for decades.

One easy way to measure your team's service quality is to ask your clients how they actually feel about your team's service work. What better way to measure your metrics than to personally answer phone calls from your clients, and ask them how your team performed. Leaders often try to place other team members between them and their customer calls, acting as a sort of buffer. I disagree, and recommend that you don't institutionalize such a buffer zone with your clients. Personally answering phone calls from your clients is a powerful reminder that you are the team leader and that you are not abdicating the responsibilities of your role. You'll likely find that most of the time your clients aren't calling to complain.

Another way to measure your service work is to proactively poll your clients and ask them how your team is doing. When you get some negative feedback, at least you have a chance to adjust before the team behaviors that caused that negative feedback become ingrained. This is effective service quality measurement and control.

The Net Promoter Score (NPS) is the most widely used method for measuring service quality. The NPS survey asks your clients only one question: "On a scale of 1-10, how likely are you to recommend us to a friend or colleague?" The answer determines your service quality score.

a. Score of 9–10 = "promoter"
b. Score of 7–8 = "neutral"
c. Score of 1–6 = "detractor"

You can look further into the NPS metric for yourself, by visiting: www.netpromoter.com

Trusted team management also requires that underperforming team members are quickly identified and either guided back to productivity—or separated from the group. If you allow an underperforming member to remain, your team will notice, and it will erode their confidence in your fairness. They'll ask privately (or not so privately): "Why is the team leader allowing the underperforming team member to drag down the entire team's performance?" We will further discuss hiring and firing of team members in another BOLDskill, so we'll leave off with this summary.

Holding regular performance reviews and making sure that all team members are fairly held accountable to attain their goals, and assuring that they have metrics they can use to self-monitor—are critical aspects to providing trusted management to your team. You can use the "Team Goal Setting Template to Achieve Accountability of Success Goals" in Appendix I to provide clear and fair goal visibility for your team members.

Here's what happens if you leave a trusted management void on your team:

• In a highly competitive service economy, you can't rely on subjective measurements or leave it up to your customers to tell you that they received unfocused and poor quality service from your team. If you do, you risk being quickly replaced by your competitors. Just look at what happened to the U.S. auto industry in the 1990s and early 2000s as discussed above.

- The opposite of a trusted management status is "arbitrary, unfair and ineffective." Have you ever worked for such a manager? If so, I bet your team became confused and demoralized as it failed in its objectives. Ideas are always questioned, fingers are quick to point to those who are to blame, and so decisions are debated endlessly while the team stagnates.

- If the team leader puts up barriers to his accessibility, and appoints another on the team to answer for service quality issues, then he has effectively abdicated his trusted management group governance role to someone else. When clients or senior management want to discuss service quality, this team leader may find that it's their team member and not the team leader who is being consulted. It's a sure way to get replaced as team leader, or to lose clients to a former employee who is seen as the guardian of service quality.

- Allowing ineffective team members to remain on the team will reduce the team's ability to achieve its goals, and makes the team leader seem arbitrary. Your team will not trust your management decisions about their careers if you get a reputation of "coddling" some employees while holding others to a high performance standard. It is difficult to fire people, but sometimes it must be done—and done quickly.

Examples of group governance role abdication thinking

The scenarios below are the most common "group governance role abdication statements" by a team leader that can cause a top performing company to *quickly* go out of business, or cause a once high-performing team to sputter:

> *"I'm not a good leader or manager, but everyone on*
> *my team is self-motivated—so it doesn't matter."*

Some people in leadership positions insist that they are not good leaders or managers; they see themselves as only very good at performing a technical or operational role. This includes senior engineers who are promoted based on their superior technical expertise. They may use their perceived or real leadership inadequacy to justify hiring these positions too early in the company's existence, delegating the group governance roles to other team members, or denying their importance for the team's performance.

If you're a company owner, hiring professional managers for these group governance positions too early, before your company has the revenues to support them while paying yourself (the owner) a fair salary, will lead to a financial crisis far earlier than you ever imagined. A company that is at or below the breakeven point does not have the cash flow to pay for professional leadership or management positions; these are roles the owner must fill until his company is viable.

As the owner, resolve to yourself from the start of your business to perform all three critical group governance roles as well as you're able, until you at least achieve breakeven success—and then some. Some people will reject this advice and still succeed, and that's fine, but my advice is based on what you need to do to be reliably repeatable. Hiring too early for critical group governance positions, diminishing their importance or ignoring them altogether, are behaviors correlated with team failure and group chaos.

If you're leading a corporate team, you may believe that one or more of these group governance roles are not important for establishing and maintaining a highly successful team. If so, you may quietly diminish their importance or even vocally declare that you don't think they're important for your team's success. "Besides," you may think, "isn't everyone on my team self-motivated?" This kind of reasoning is sadly misguided. Your team will naturally seek out the group governance needs that they have—and if you haven't provided a way for them to feel ownership in the team's mission, follow an inspired leader, and trust the team's management—then they'll improvise to fill any voids. This kind of group governance role abdication results in a wandering team focus, group conflict, and less-than optimal performances.

We all give our best performances when we can focus our talents on achieving specific, articulated team objectives, coordinated with the efforts of the other people on our team, who are all accountable to and aware of looming deadlines, motivated by a shared BOLD purpose, and cheered on by an inspiring and trusted team leader.

> *"The truth is, I just don't have the energy to*
> *continue to 'fight the good fight' anymore."*

The burden of running your company or managing your team may wear you down, and you may come to believe that it's best to conserve your energy for those "unforeseen events" that always seem to take over to dictate your team's direction and destiny. You may feel that you just don't have the energy, patience, capital, or the will to continue to fight or provide conscious group role governance. But if you start to feel hopeless and pessimistic, you can learn to regain or bolster your optimism and take positive actions to reset your team's trajectory. One method to do this is by "developing your inner voice," a voice of reason that can rally you back to feeling optimistic and hopeful—giving you renewed energy to fight for your team's success.

To do this, go back to the "ABCDE Exercise for Identifying and Overcoming Fear" that we discussed in a prior chapter and included in Appendix F of this book. You can use it to help you develop an inner voice of reason for yourself—learning how to dispute fears with facts, and increase your feelings of optimism and hope. This should help you develop a renewable source of energy when you feel you're running low.

"I feel inadequate to perform the group governance roles."

We all have days when we feel inadequate, yet we still have to perform our critical group roles. Take a few slow, deep breaths. Close your eyes and envision your most confident self. Remember the many difficult situations you've faced in the past—and how you overcame all obstacles to succeed. Ask lots of questions and let the other person talk more. Take notes. Then look the other person in the eyes and tell them "We can help you," or "We'll get the problem fixed." Then make an appointment for a date in the next few days so you can gather your thoughts and prepare a thoughtful solution. It's that simple, but it's never easy. What is very easy is to slowly abdicate the group governance roles to your senior team members, while you hide fearfully behind a closed office door.

If you can perform your critical group governance roles, even on days that you feel vulnerable, then you're on your way to building an unstoppable Surging Team. But If you let your team members perform the group governance roles, you'll cause confusion on your team and almost guarantee that you'll be seen as "ineffective." This can lead to your being replaced as the team leader or losing control of your company's culture, if not the company itself. Your team will find their own leaders, and will develop a group culture without your guidance.

It takes practice to gain mastery and become an expert at providing ownership engagement, inspired leadership, and trusted management. Malcolm Gladwell, in *Outliers: The Story of Success*, estimates that it takes 10,000 hours or 5 years of full-time work to gain mastery at any task. As the team leader, accept these three critical group governance roles as yours alone to perform, and resolve to master them, no matter how long it takes you.

BOLD takeaways

- The company owner or appointed team leader must intentionally perform the three group governance roles of: 1. providing a way for your team members to feel ownership in the team's mission (ownership engagement); 2. feeling they're following an inspired leader (inspired leadership); and 3. trust that the team leader will provide fair management (trusted management).

- If you don't intentionally provide these three critical group governance roles, then your team members will improvise to fill any voids. Group governance role abdication by the team leader results in a wandering team focus, group conflict, and less than optimal performances. The group will fill the three group governance roles among themselves, without your direction.

- We give our best performances when we can focus our talents on achieving specific, articulated team objectives, coordinated with the efforts of other people on our team, who are all accountable to and aware of looming deadlines, motivated by a shared BOLD purpose, and cheered on by an inspiring and trusted team leader. Intentionally developing your group governance roles assures that the team will give its best performances each and every time you need them.

- Your clients, your company, and your team members will notice who is providing the inspired leadership and trusted management they need. If it isn't coming from the appointed team leader, then that leader is in danger of losing his team's leadership role and potentially his clients to anyone who steps in to fill this void. This is the number one way that an established small business quickly goes out of business—or a team leader gets fired.

BOLDskill 5

BOLDLY work to increase your team's positive collective spirit

Suppose you picked the top guys from high school
and gave them world-class military training. Even so,
there's no way they'd fight as good as us. It's not just
training, it's a feeling we have of how to work together.
— BING WEST, FROM *ONE MILLION STEPS*,
QUOTING MARINE PFC JEFFREY RUSHTON

If you changed the venue from war to business, do the words spoken by Marine PFC Rushton represent how your company or your team feels about its ability to compete? A U.S. Marine platoon depends on their ability to coordinate together to deliver disruptive power to overcome obstacles—and they are world renown for their devastating effectiveness. If you challenge them, they'll work together relentlessly until they move past you or through you, to achieve their team objective. The same should apply to your company's or team's ability to summon collaboration, co-creativity, and persistence in order to overcome obstacles. Does your company or team have the "there's no way they'd fight as good as us" feeling of how to work together to succeed?

If BOLDskill 1 is about how team leaders need to recognize and seize opportunities to lead their team, BOLDskill 5 is the corollary, specifically designed to assure that your team members, too, are mentally ready and empowered to perform. To achieve astounding success with your team, your team members must feel as PFC Rushton felt about his Marine platoon.

Developing the team's ability to summon proactive change strategies to achieve goals

Like a Marine platoon, your company team must develop a feeling of being relentless and devastatingly effective, no matter what it takes, in order for your company to succeed in an increasingly competitive marketplace. Generating success is proactive work, and there are two kinds of proactive strategies available to you:

1. *Evolutionary change*—the kind that evolves slowly and steadily, according to a plan
2. *Revolutionary change*—the kind that deviates from the plan to bring a disruptive power that allows you to catapult past or through unforeseen obstacles

As a corporate team leader or business owner, you need to employ both evolutionary and revolutionary proactive change strategies in order to gain the success edge over your competition. You can usually find the roadmap for evolutionary change in any company's business plan, organizational chart, and operations manual. However, companies don't always succeed through planned, evolutionary change alone. Their business plan will not be able to anticipate all the situations that require innovative, outside-the-box thinking in order to continue on their mission. Sometimes in the face of a success barrier, a team needs to regroup and use revolutionary change strategies to move past it. But can your company depend on revolutionary change automatically "showing up" when it's needed? How does a company summon this other, more devastating, type of change potential?

Revolutionary change becomes available when your team develops a "powerfully positive collective spirit." By this, I mean that your team has the ability to go "off script" and find innovative ways to solve a vexing problem on their way to achieve a team success objective. Once a powerfully positive collective spirit develops inside a group, it becomes an unseen and indomitable reservoir for revolutionary change—delivering power that can mobilize creativity and innovative thinking for the purpose of overcoming obstacles.

A Marine platoon at war is an example of a Surging Team that sometimes must rely on revolutionary change strategies when their original plan gets them stalled. Anyone who's experienced the powerfully positive collective spirit that develops among platoon members, a spirit that produces innovative heroic acts and bold gambles when the team needs it in order to win—will remember it for a lifetime. Can a business unit achieve a similar type of boldness and effectiveness at summoning innovation and delivering revolutionary change when it's needed to achieve their goals? I believe they can.

Diagramming the dynamics of an unstoppable Surging Team

The Collective Spirit Diagram on the next page demonstrates the relationship between the various key team elements and the team's ability to summon innovative thinking and use it to deliver revolutionary change.

As the diagram shows, there are several dynamics that happen simultaneously to result in increasing a team's positive collective spirit. A team with a powerfully positive collective spirit uses the team leader's inspired leadership and team brainstorming to produce innovations that allow the team to deliver revolutionary change when it's needed—like a wedge to break through barriers —to achieve the team's success goals.

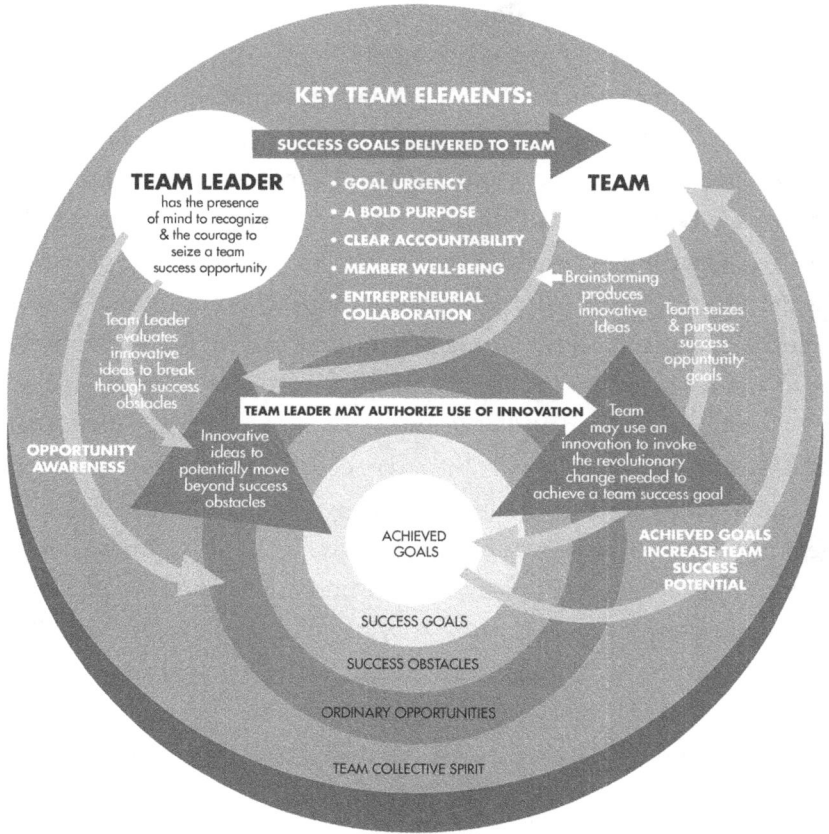

KEY TEAM ELEMENTS:

SUCCESS GOALS DELIVERED TO TEAM

TEAM LEADER
has the presence
of mind to recognize
& the courage to
seize a team
success opportunity

- **GOAL URGENCY**
- **A BOLD PURPOSE**
- **CLEAR ACCOUNTABILITY**
- **MEMBER WELL-BEING**
- **ENTREPRENEURIAL COLLABORATION**

TEAM

Brainstorming
produces
innovative
ideas

Team seizes
& pursues:
success
opportunity
goals

Team Leader
evaluates
innovative
ideas to break
through success
obstacles

TEAM LEADER MAY AUTHORIZE USE OF INNOVATION

Team
may use an
innovation to invoke
the revolutionary
change needed to
achieve a team success goal

OPPORTUNITY AWARENESS

Innovative
ideas to
potentially move
beyond success
obstacles

ACHIEVED GOALS
INCREASE TEAM
SUCCESS
POTENTIAL

ACHIEVED
GOALS

SUCCESS GOALS

SUCCESS OBSTACLES

ORDINARY OPPORTUNITIES

TEAM COLLECTIVE SPIRIT

A team's positive collective spirit produces innovative thinking
and revolutionary change potential

Let's look in detail at the various dynamics in the diagram.

The concentric circles

The outer circle represents where your team's collective spirit lives. Drilling down, the next circle is where ordinary opportunities live—your team is surrounded by these ordinary opportunities. Inside of ordinary opportunities are success obstacles. Success obstacles are what surround the next circle in the diagram—success goals. Once a team leader identifies an ordinary opportunity, and chooses it as a success goal for his team—the team has to somehow get past the success obstacles in order to achieve their goal. The team can then breakthrough to the innermost circle—achieved goals.

What if the team can't break through their success obstacles, by just following their business plan? That's where innovative thinking and revolutionary change strategies come in—and they're represented by the "wedges" in the diagram, which we will discuss below. A team that can conceive of innovative ideas, and then choose one and use it to break through a seemingly impenetrable success obstacle—is a team that has just delivered effective revolutionary change.

Arrows in the diagram

On the far left is the "opportunity awareness arrow;" it originates from the team leader and ends in the circle that contains "ordinary opportunities." An effective team leader becomes aware of ordinary opportunities, and strategically seizes one to present to his team in the form of a success goal. This chosen goal is represented by the horizontal arrow across the top of the diagram that moves from the team leader to the team, entitled "success goals delivered to the team." The team leader uses the key team elements of goal urgency, team BOLD purpose, clear accountability, increasing team member well-being, and entrepreneurial collaboration—to deliver a success goal to his team. An effective leader is aware of the key team elements, and accepts the responsibility of developing her mastery at building these key team elements. We'll review these key team elements later in this chapter.

Look now at the arrow on the far right of the diagram, labeled "achieved goals increase team success potential." Every time a team achieves a success goal, it increases the team's success potential—and this reinforces the team's belief that "they'll always win." It's critical to developing a Surging Team that the leader assures that each time he presents a success goal, his team eventually achieves it. You can also see that the arrow entitled "achieved goals increase team success potential" ends in the outer circle of "Team Collective Spirit," on its way to becoming part of the Team. Achieved goals increase a team's positive collective spirit.

The wedge shapes

As previously noted, the two wedges represent innovative thinking and revolutionary change strategies, respectively. Consider first the wedge on the left of the diagram, entitled "innovative ideas to potentially move beyond success obstacles." Coming into this wedge are two arrows. On the right is an arrow originating from the "Team," and that arrow is labeled "brainstorming produces innovative ideas." On the left is an arrow originating from the "team leader," entitled "Team Leader evaluates innovative ideas to break through success obstacles."

Leveraging a key team element of "entrepreneurial collaboration," and utilizing the "team brainstorming technique" when her team is confronted by a success obstacle, the team leader solicits ideas from her team to identify innovative ways to get past the obstacle.

However, it is solely up to the team leader to determine if the team will utilize one of the innovative ideas sourced from the team brainstorming session—and by doing so, engage disruptive, revolutionary change as a strategy to get past the success obstacle. This decision is sublime and may have significant organizational repercussions, which is why I insist it is a decision that only the team leader can make.

Deciding to deviate from the evolutionary change strategy as laid out in your company business plan is a BOLD and risky decision. Bureaucracies naturally resist unplanned change, and the leader of a Surging Team will need to be prepared to negotiate with all the affected teams inside the company in order to get them to accept this revolutionary change strategy. The gravity of this decision is the reason for the horizontal arrow in the middle of the diagram, the one titled "Team Leader may authorize innovation." It connects the two wedges. On the left is the wedge that represents the team's innovative ideas; on the right is the wedge that represents an innovative idea chosen by the team leader—an innovation that will be used to deliver revolutionary change to break through or catapult her team over a success obstacle. A Surging Team always achieves their success goals, so the team leader will sometimes need to use a revolutionary change strategy to make certain her team retains an unwavering belief in their eventual success.

The "Team" circle

In the top right of the diagram is the team circle. Follow the arrow coming out of the right side of the Team circle, entitled "Team seizes & pursues success opportunity goals." Notice that this arrow flows through the "invoke revolutionary change" wedge and comes out the bottom of this wedge and penetrates all the concentric circles—to end in "Achieved Goals." Once the Team Leader chooses an opportunity and presents her Team with a success goal, the team seizes this success goal and pursues its achievement.

Again, the Team may, or may not, need to use a revolutionary change strategy, but if they do, it should only be authorized by the leader. Most success goals can be achieved through the use of the evolutionary change strategies outlined in the company's business plan and represented by the company's stated policies and procedures. But in a competitive marketplace, there will be goals that are highly desired by multiple companies, and this is when the team with the most highly developed positive collective spirit will utilize an innovation to invoke the revolutionary change needed to win.

CREATING URGENCY

During their infantry training, the U. S. Marines practice throwing dummy grenades and then running for cover to prepare for the blast. To pass the grenade throwing part of their training, they have to detonate a live grenade on their last throw. Afterwards, the Marine instructors pointed out to their new Marines that they had run twice as far on their last, live throw. There just wasn't any urgency until they knew it was "live."

The five key team elements to achieving success goals

The team leader has the responsibility to develop and utilize the following five key team elements when presenting success goals to his team:

1. Goal urgency
2. Team BOLD purpose
3. Clear accountability
4. Increasing team member well-being
5. Entrepreneurial collaboration

Let's look at the key team elements, one at a time.

Team element 1: Goal urgency

In business, goal urgency usually comes in the form of deadlines that must be met. Deadlines should not be arbitrary, held closely, or kept secret. Goals need to be carefully evaluated by the team leader and vetted for potential before they are accepted as a team success goal. A Surging Team must believe that they'll always achieve their goals, on time, and within budget. Once a success goal is accepted by the team leader, it must also be presented with its deadline and a methodology for measuring whether the goal is achieved. The entire team needs to understand the goal and commit to achieving it. A goal without a deadline *and* a method to measure its successful achievement is not a goal at all—it's only a distraction and a source of team frustration. In order to have urgency, the deadline has to be universally known and preferably published and updated constantly—accompanied by the current measurement of the team's progress in its attainment.

Team element 2: Developing a team BOLD purpose

Since this is the subject of BOLDskill 3, we won't repeat that explanation here, but I will emphasize that when a team adopts a BOLD purpose, one that is greater than their own individual objectives, it becomes a powerful force in assuring that the team maintains an attitude of doing whatever it takes to win. The team emphasizes and reinforces its BOLD purpose through telling team success stories that exemplify it.

Team element 3: Clear accountability

This is accomplished when the Team Leader assures that all appropriate members of the team understand and internalize their role in guaranteeing that the team success goal is achieved. A team success goal can't be achieved when it is solely held by the team leader and not delegated appropriately to her team. There is no "finger pointing" when clear accountability is present, because it is well publicized throughout the company as to who owns the goal. You can use the "Team Goal Setting Template to Achieve Accountability of Success Goals" in Appendix I to provide clear and fair goal visibility for your team members.

Team element 4: Increasing team member well-being

We discussed the components of PERMA in BOLDskill#1, so in this chapter we'll just remind you that higher PERMA scores are equated with stronger feelings of happiness and well-being. One way to accomplish "increasing team member well-being" is to teach your team members how to use their individual signature strengths most effectively to further the team's goal attainment.

As the company owner or team leader, do you know what your team members' individual character strengths are? Are you leveraging those strengths, or are you still trying to help your team members improve their weaknesses? Recent research has shown that only one-third of team leaders can identify the signature character strengths of their team members. Most team leaders are still focused on helping their team members improve by "identifying and fixing their weaknesses." Think about all the performance reviews you've been part of—most of them seemed focused on finding something—anything that you need to improve on. In fact, a performance review was often incomplete without finding something for an employee to improve.

Recent research, however, has debunked this "identify and fix your weakness" management style, and instead supports the "identify, create awareness of, and leverage what you're already strongest at" as a vastly superior, alternative management style.

Interestingly, Dr. Martin Seligman's research into happiness and well-being—and his subsequent PERMA model to measure and increase both—are now being used by the United States military to improve the positive collective spirit of military teams. Our military saw and accepted the evidence provided by Seligman's research on individual well-being, and it now recognizes that happier platoons and military units perform better. The military has implemented Seligman's findings and are now including "the proven ability to raise the PERMA happiness and well-being scores of their units" as a major component for officer-rank promotions. It turns out that our analogy between a platoon and a work team wasn't such a stretch after all!

When each team member is aware of their individual strengths—and the team leader is equally aware of the individual strengths of each team member—the conditions for feelings of well-being and happiness are present. A team with high member PERMA scores fights better, experiences improved performance, and innovates better when confronted with a barrier to success.

Team happiness and fulfillment scores are so important to team success that team leaders must be held accountable for those scores. I propose here that any team leader who is unwilling or unable to raise their team's PERMA scores, should be replaced. An unstoppable Surging Team depends on a leader who understands this and works toward achieving higher PERMA scores, increasing feelings of well-being, and developing the positive collective spirit of her team. Achievement is the "A" in PERMA, so goal achievement itself raises the team members' feelings of well-being.

Team element 5: Entrepreneurial collaboration

In his classic book *Think and Grow Rich*, Napoleon Hill describes a "mastermind group" as a group of peers who meet regularly for the purpose of pooling their ideas, encouragement, and support to produce innovations and achieve significant financial success for each member of the group. Hill proposes, "Every mind needs friendly contact with other minds, for food of expansion and growth."

A mastermind peer group can be an effective tool to hold peer members accountable to each other and to their goals, so they can achieve astonishing results. A successful mastermind group will develop a powerful "collective spirit" that has the potential to inspire positive, disruptive revolutionary change power. I have found that one of the best ways for a company to develop a "mastermind peer group" culture among their internal teams—is through brainstorming sessions. I'm sure you know the term, but to be clear, these are meetings intended to consciously develop a list of creative and innovative options from a team of people with a stake in its success. Brainstorming allows a company to tap ideas from within, and open themselves up to internal change. There is one basic rule during a brainstorming session: "No idea criticism" during the session—just let the ideas flow and do the evaluating at another time.

I call the idea-generating power that results from a peer mastermind group or through effective team brainstorming "entrepreneurial collaboration." It is one of the key team elements that you must cultivate. Entrepreneurial collaboration is a powerful culture that encourages both the use of known best practices as well as the consideration of innovative ideas, in order to allow the team to quickly navigate around barriers that are preventing successful goal achievement. Innovative ideas emerge from a team that has all five key team elements, and then engages in brainstorming in order to solve a problem. Surging Teams embrace a culture of entrepreneurial collaboration because it allows the team to reach beyond the accepted methodologies of the company in their pursuit of goal achievement and success. When your team develops a culture of entrepreneurial collaboration, they have the ability to identify innovative solutions to solve complex problems that can't be overcome by merely examining the operations manual or following known rules or best practices.

NASA's Mars Land Rover Team of scientists was challenged to come up with a way to slow down the space capsule that carried the Land Rover to the surface of Mars. Given the speed that it would be travelling, the landing impact would destroy the craft and its cargo. The team held a brainstorming session to come up with ideas on how to slow down the landing craft enough to have a chance to land without destroying itself on impact with the Mars surface. One of the team's constraints was that they had a limited budget that prevented them from inventing some expensive solution. After many complex and expensive possible options, a team member suggested "using a parachute." Sounds crazy right? I mean, a parachute on Mars?! In the end, it was indeed a parachute system that was used to successfully land a Rover on Mars.

Bureaucracies resist revolutionary change

As a team leader, it's your responsibility to fight for the conditions that will nurture innovation among your team in their effort to

TRACKING YOUR TEAM'S STRENGTHS

Here is how you track and utilize your team signature strengths to ensure you can maximize them. This is based on identifying and measuring the components of well-being and happiness found in the PERMA model.

1. First, have each of your team members take the free VIA Character Survey to identify their top five "signature strengths." You can find the VIA Survey at authentichappiness.org or on our website at boldbreak.com/start-surging-now.

2. Individually review each team member's VIA survey results with them, and make sure they're aware of their top signature strengths—and that they know you're aware of them, too.

3. Next, create an organization chart that includes each team member's top five character strengths, so that each time you see your team members' names, you're also reminded of their signature strengths. Keep this chart handy and make it a habit to consult it often as you plan your team's strategies and tactics. You can use the Signature Strength's Org Chart in Appendix B of this book to keep your team's signature strength's at the ready.

achieve their goals. However, bureaucracies thrive on procedures and usually attempt to crush creativity and innovation—compelling the team to adhere to the established procedures, even ineffective ones. The "not invented here" syndrome is alive and well at corporate offices. Sometimes ideas coming from the senior executive team may be considered "innovations," while ideas coming from the teams that are actually closer to delivering the company's products and services are often considered "operating out of compliance" or "coloring outside the lines." I've had senior executive team members openly refer to my team members as "pirates," plundering corporate resources. This was meant unkindly, and worked to increase corporate scrutiny on us in an effort to slow down our revolutionary change tactics.

There were hard feelings and jealousy among some corporate executives in the companies I've been in. They expressed resentment in executive committee meetings about my team's "deviance from standard operating procedures," and my "overuse of company resources." I knew of this because I had reliable sources in those meetings. "Why the hell are we giving the Dining Program that kind of budget? Why are we letting our flagship services atrophy, while we fund a boondoggle?" But even with this jealousy and opposition, as long as my team continued to succeed in our objectives, we were not formally asked to discontinue our innovative business tactics, although there was some budget tightening as a result of these protests. I accepted this as a backhanded compliment from my executive peers, and resolved to find even more creative ways to operate in a budget-strapped environment. Regardless, we kept up our unconventional drive to success.

Strict adherence to current procedures is the way to deliver average, mediocre results—and average results usually don't equate to marketplace success. If you work for a business that does not allow for innovations from the ranks of its employees, then you can expect to see a more mediocre company and mediocre team results—because that's what resistance to innovation and change usually fosters—mediocrity.

What if your company will not allow for any "deviations" from their operations manual? If this is your company culture, then keep a low profile if you find they are opposing reasonable innovations that you and your team introduce to achieve your team's goals. It's better to follow the old adage of asking for forgiveness rather than asking for permission. What exactly are "reasonable innovations?" The boundary between "reasonable" and "outrageous" is a little blurry in my book, but I'm sometimes described as a maverick. I know that blurriness is distressing to some people who always want to know the "rules." But better-than-average chances for breakthrough success are contained in that blurriness.

The less-blurry and more defined the company operating environment is, the less tolerance there is for innovation. Consider philosopher Immanuel Kant's "Universal Law," and how it might apply to your company: "Always act in such a way that [. . .] the maxim of your act become[s] a Universal Law that all can also follow."

Remember: Whatever the company allows for your team to do, they must allow for all to do. Relaxing a policy for your team could get difficult for the company to manage. That's why most companies are very selective about what they include in their official operations guidelines, even if they know there are "better" operating tactics being used inside the company (better = resulting in more and faster profitability). Thus, as team leader, adopt Kant's Universal Law as your own. In a "blurry" environment, act responsibly with company resources, mindful that every other team leader in your company is watching you—or soon will be.

This is why it is only the team leaders that should be allowed to authorize the use of revolutionary change through the implementation of an innovative solution designed to get past a success obstacle. Only the team leaders should have the authority and the potential political influence within the company to successfully introduce and integrate a revolutionary change company-wide. But it won't be easy.

Examples of identifying innovative ideas using brainstorming

A "company resources" innovation sourced via team brainstorming by my GE team

While leading my corporate team at GE and developing a national discount dining program, we collected a rich database of restaurant credit card transactions. The business intelligence potential contained in this database was exciting—and actionable information gleaned from this data was soon in high demand by our marketing department. Marketing wanted to predict the next dining behavior by our restaurant program members, and use that information to increase program revenues.

The problem that quickly developed, however, was that the business intelligence requested by our marketing department outstripped our IT team's ability to deliver it in both a timely and actionable manner. Marketing believed they could vastly increase our membership base, and thus increase our revenues, if they had access to better and more timely information.

I pulled my team together for a brainstorming session to consider solutions to this dilemma. One suggestion was to put more pressure on our IT department to prioritize our division's business intelligence requests. That was what our IT department would expect us to do—and, of course, they had the option of approving or denying our escalation requests based on all the work they had from GE's many other divisions. In brainstorming with my team for more ideas, it was suggested that we again seek to outsource our business intelligence technology needs, a solution that would not involve our internal IT department.

As an alternative though, a member of my operations team suggested that we develop a "shadow file" reporting system that would feed us a copy of the credit card transactions as they came in. This option did not involve our internal IT department or require an outsourced technology partner. We could then use this shadow file reporting system to develop a custom business intelligence reporting system—one that would be completely operated and managed by our team.

These were the best solutions our meeting surfaced, so we ended our brainstorming and considered them carefully. Putting pressure on our IT department to prioritize our business intelligence requests was ruled out, as our IT team had recently finished developing our production computer system to collect these trans-actions efficiently. IT had other GE internal corporate clients who were waiting for their turn to get their own IT support. Besides, the business intelligence requests from marketing were constant; there would be no end to their need for prioritizing our projects with IT. We also ruled out the outsourcing option, as we had just spent the last four months of GE's IT resources to bring the transaction data collection system in-house. The third option, developing our own shadow file and using it to analyze actionable information for marketing, seemed to be the best way to go. The big question was, did we have the bandwidth and ability on our team to take on the effort of maintaining and delivering business intelligence services to our marketing department? I looked around the table for an answer.

My team members each had that smiling-at-each-other-know-ingly and head-nodding look. Our team had gained a reputation as innovative problem solvers, and they felt that they'd always win—and this was another opportunity to prove it again. In the end, our shadow-file business intelligence system worked, and marketing was able to use the resulting information to grow our revenues. Eventually, I went on to lead the business intelligence efforts at the company that would later purchase our GE division.

Another example of innovation sourced through team brainstorming from my GE days

We were struggling with our quality assurance efforts. Our sales team was selling restaurants to join our program, and they were delivering new restaurant contracts from cities all around the country. These contracts were all sent to one place—my operations team. The first problem was that our team member who was re-sponsible for the first task of "doing the data entry work" to get the new restaurants entered into our computer system, had fallen woefully behind. Even when a restaurant was entered into our system, there were many mistakes in the data entry process that had to be corrected, and once the data entry was finally done, then the restaurant was handed off to the next team member to work with the restaurant's credit card system to be sure we were collecting dining transactions by our members. This effort of assuring the new restaurant was sending credit card transactions into our collection system was also woefully behind. I pulled my team together for a brainstorming session.

"I need another person to help me get these contracts entered into the computer system," said Steve, "just give me another person to help." This was idea #1, the obvious one of "just get me more help."

"There are too many data fields required in the data entry process," said another team member, "can't we eliminate some of these data fields?" This became idea #2, the perennial "cut some work out."

"What if we didn't have so many silos?" said another team member. "What if each of us was responsible for the complete lifecycle of a restaurant in our program—from data entry to data collection?" This was idea #3, the "let's radically change how things get done."

Can you guess which idea my team decided to move forward with? Of course, it was idea #3, and it revolutionized our operations department. I totally redesigned the objectives of each of our team members, and they *each* became responsible for the complete restaurant lifecycle for a specific group of cities. Instead of data entry and data collection silos, we had operations regional managers who were each responsible for the entire range of tasks to bring a new restaurant into a participating status with our program. Job satisfaction among my team went through the roof, team productivity reached the highest levels we'd ever seen, and our restaurant program continued to grow.

A "virtual office" innovation, gained through brainstorming
during my franchise business ownership

The biggest problem facing a new business owner is the limited amount of capital available to get the business started. Should I spend my limited capital on leasing an office or could I figure out a system for delivering my services from our home offices—and work without a central office?

In my case, this decision not only involved a major recurring cost item for me as the owner (rent and utilities), it was also a major component in determining the quality of life for everyone working for my franchise computer services company. Leaving home each day and then returning later that night is a major lifestyle commitment.

Early in my franchise company's formation, I held a meeting with my team in a conference room at the local chamber of commerce. I posed the question to them: "My franchise system recommends that I lease office space. Should we lease a central office, or do you want to learn how we can deliver our computer services from our individual home offices?"

We had a robust brainstorming discussion. Some team members had never worked from home, and feared the loss of effective communications with their team members who wouldn't be within "shouting distance." Although they liked the freedom of working from home, they feared being "out of the loop." They didn't say no; they were just afraid of "losing something important." Other team members saw it as a chance to have a "work-from-anywhere" lifestyle, and it made the job opportunity my company offered seem more attractive. Then a team member pointed out that we could always "meet at the chamber of commerce every Monday, just like we were doing now, and spend a few hours in a face-to-face team meeting."

I'm sure you can guess what we ended up doing. It didn't take long before even our Monday chamber meetings became a conference call that didn't require being face-to-face. From that day forward, we set up the business so that my entire team could work from home or anywhere that had a wireless Internet connection.

In the short run, this decision, made through a brainstorming session by my early team, became a key element in preserving our precious start-up capital and bringing in talented and motivated employees for less-than-market compensation. It may have been the single biggest decision contributing to my company's financial success. My employees all felt they had a hand in making the virtual office decision, they enjoyed their freedom from having to go to a central office, and it added to our positive collective team spirit.

In the long run, our experience with a virtual office also surprised me. It turns out that most people work *harder* and *longer* from home than people who commute to an office. This happens because the line that separates when work starts and when your personal life begins gets blurred when you work from home. Home office workers find that they have to consciously make an effort to put their work down, whereas if you work from an office, five or six p.m. is usually the cue to start your personal life for the evening.

The barriers to success in a virtual office are mainly management problems—both the attitude of the manager and the ability of the team to maintain effective communications. We used group texting and emailing to give our team a sense of working together in a physical office, constantly giving other team members a sense of what everyone was working on. It also allowed us to leverage the Hawthorne Effect by allowing everyone (especially me, the company owner) to see who was responding to a service call and when that service call was completed. When people know their work is able to be monitored, they tend to perform better. "Visibility" was the key to our effective virtual office. Once everyone understood the virtual office rules, knew that I could monitor them, and that I'd enforce the office rules (like start times), then things began to hum along quite well.

Our "virtual office" decision also opened the door to some highly motivated, fantastic employees who had the talent my company needed, but at that point in their lives they couldn't have taken an office job away from home for 8-10 hours per day. These same people were willing to work for less than market rates and forgo the other extended-benefit expectations of a larger employer—precisely because they found in us a job that allowed them the flexibility to work from home. Due to our successful virtual office strategy, I was able to assemble a far more motivated and less-costly team than many of my marketplace competitors. One of my virtual office employees even purchased my company from me when I was ready to sell it.

IN BUSINESS, RESISTANCE TO CHANGE SIGNALS ORGANIZATIONAL DOOM

A recent article in *Time Magazine,* "Innovate or Die: Lessons from Apple, Google, and Toyota," points out that teams must be ready and willing to embrace change. The article asks the question, "So how do successful companies stay relevant?" and answers it with, "The best way to succeed in the long run is to be open to the change and to tap the ideas from people within the organization. The problem occurs when firms fight the change and cling to the old business. " As Frank Herbert pointed out in *Heretics of Dune:* "Bureaucracy destroys initiative. There is little that bureaucrats hate more than innovation, especially innovation that produces better results than the old routines. Improvements always make those at the top of the heap look inept [. . .] When bureaucrats successfully fight needed internal change, and cling to the old business, then the doom is certain."

The cost of not using the innovative ideas
sourced by team brainstorming

The team leaders of an innovative company must encourage, accept, and provide a process for rapid assimilation of team-sourced innovations and new best practices that result from brainstorming sessions. If the company leaders fail to do this, they break the delicate link between the team members' ideas and efforts—and their reward of feeling that their ideas and efforts were used and directly contributed to both their team and personal successes. If this delicate link is broken, the team will cease risking their ideas, and they will limit their efforts to only those required by "following the operations manual."

Here's an example from my experience of how one key technology executive at GE had limited both himself and our entire corporate IT team because he only considered ideas found by "following the departmental operations manual." This situation is actually the background to the story I told you about right at the beginning of the book in the chapter "What is a Surging Team?" —the day I met with Bill, the VP of IT who was so incredulous that my team had accomplished something he had refused to do. This is how we arrived at Bill asking me "How the heck did you do that?"

The story began months earlier when I thought I was putting together a peer brainstorming meeting between Bill (head of IT), Jim (head of marketing), and me (operations) about our ideas for a new discount dining program. Jim and I had already talked about some possibilities, and we sought to meet with Bill so he'd get familiar with them and contribute his own to see if we could source some innovative thinking. After we sat down, Jim explained the dynamic new product idea he was envisioning. In response, Bill looked across the table and asked, "Did you fill out an Information System Services Request (ISSR) form?"

These were the first words that the VP in charge of our company's computer systems asked us. Jim, who was a newly hired marketing director, looked confused, of course. He had never heard of this "ISSR" form, and it seemed an odd response to the compelling new product presentation he'd just made. Bill then looked over at me and I knew what he was thinking. He already felt overwhelmed with keeping *his* (i.e., the company's) computer systems running, and he had no time to participate in or encourage creativity or innovation, even if it would lead to profits for GE. He had lapsed into "following the operations manual" mode, and was using a "missing form" as an effective defense against ambiguous "computer use requests" for help from his team. If the "computer user" couldn't specifically define the need, and articulate that need inside the pre-printed spaces on the ISSR form—then Bill would not consider the request for computer services to be legitimate.

"Bill, this is a brainstorming session, we're not asking for support yet—just your ideas on how that computer support might look, given the interesting new product ideas that marketing is presenting here," I futilely explained.

Jim didn't know that I used to work for Bill in the IT department. I was offered and accepted a management position in operations, mainly because I intimately knew how to use our complex computer systems—since I helped write the code and maintained the company's computer programs. I was effectively the liaison between IT and all our various "computer user" groups. But this VP of Information Systems resented the fact that I used "insider IT knowledge" to creatively assist user groups like Marketing to expand the use of our company's computer systems, sometimes in ways they were not originally intended.

"If you don't have a completed ISSR, then there's nothing to talk about, and this meeting is over until you submit a completed form," Bill said conclusively. Jim and I offered only a pleading look as our response, so Bill got up and left the conference room.

"What do we do now?" said Jim. He was now worried about his project (and was probably concerned for his new job as well.)

"I've got an idea Jim, but I need a couple of weeks. Don't worry, we'll make this happen. I'll be in touch," and on that note, we parted.

I spent the next few weeks developing a plan, and negotiating with an outside vendor to perform the IT support we needed. In a few weeks, our outside IT vendor demonstrated a working proto- type of our new service for Jim and me. Excited, we called another meeting several weeks later with Bill. We didn't have an ISSR form filled out, but we did demonstrate our prototype for him.

"How the heck did you do that?" Bill asked, bewildered at our working prototype. And you recall the story from here—when I told Bill that we had used an outside vendor to complete the IT work. I knew we would eventually need Bill's IT group to actively help us, but they had left us no choice—our IT team had lost their ability to brainstorm and source innovative ideas from within, and they had become an obstacle to success. The cost of not practicing innovative thinking is to lose the ability to do so.

The next five years saw the explosive growth of our company's new dining program. I won the "Chairman's Challenge Award for Outstanding Intrapreneurship" for my efforts. Some people never got over our internal conflict. Each day was a new battle, inside my own company. Even with this recognition of my team's work, some among the old guard fought us at every opportunity. They just didn't understand how to innovate or accept that sometimes it is needed.

You can't force positive collective spirit, but you can BOLDLY work to create the conditions

The moral of the above story is that you can't "make" innovation happen. The conditions for accepting and embracing creative ideas from your peers or from your own team need to be nurtured well in advance of your need for them. I have offered you the five key team elements for developing collective spirit as a guide for you to establish those right conditions on your team. Your company's and your team's positive spirit must be consciously cultivated, so that it can be summoned precisely when needed to produce innovations necessary to drive past obstacles. I also offered you a diagram to show you the relationship between you as the team leader with your team, your goals, your key team elements, and how it all works together to generate innovation and goal achievement.

Some people like to be near the fire, but are content to remain at a slight distance and fantasize about leading. They are afraid to walk through the fire themselves and truly take their team to the pinnacles of success. That's where courage comes in. Inspired BOLD leaders, as I define them, would rather risk failure than stand forever with those "cold and timid souls who never dared and never tried," as President Theodore Roosevelt once famously said. As the business owner or team leader, it is your duty and privilege to embrace your role of nurturing and even fighting for the conditions that allow a positive collective spirit to develop on your team. It won't happen by accident; it won't happen by always following the operational procedures manual; and it won't happen without a fight, but that fight is a noble one, worthy of any battle scars you and your team receive along the way. Those scars will become your legendary stories and anecdotes that your team can repeat over a beer together, for a lifetime.

Your team deserves the opportunity to succeed. So does your company, and so do you.

The Surging Team Collective Spirit Worksheet

This worksheet is a tool you can use to help develop your team's positive collective spirit by putting it to work to solve a team problem. Use this worksheet to identify a critical team goal that's falling behind schedule, then brainstorm to identify options to get back on schedule, choose an option, and track progress until the goal is achieved. Remember: A Surging Team always meets their goals, on time and within budget.

EXERCISES TO GET YOU STARTED ON THE CONCEPTS

I have included *The Surging Team Profile* Assessment in Appendix D, so you can measure your current score as the team leader and the collective scores of your team. As you begin to master the 10 BOLDskills for Accelerated Team Success, and transform your people into an unstoppable Surging Team, measure your scores at regular intervals. Make sure they are all improving. As your scores go up, the conditions for developing a powerfully positive collective spirit among your team will also improve. If you don't measure your scores, then you'll have no idea how you and your team are doing in your quest to become an unstoppable Surging Team.

In addition to the above mentioned assessment, use *The Surging Team Collective Spirit Exercise* below, whenever you need to reinforce your team's collective spirit. A copy of this exercise is in Appendix J, so you can photocopy it and fill it out.

---

1. Have a Signature Strengths Org Chart in front of you that has the top five strengths of each of your team members (like the one provided in Appendix B).

2. What team, department, or company goals are falling behind schedule?

3. Rank the "falling behind schedule" goals by required completion date, then choose one that has the nearest completion date and/or the most urgency.

4. Make sure your team is aware of this goal, the completion date, and your budgetary constraints.

5. What metric is being used to measure progress toward this goal? If none, then create an appropriate metric and write it here.

6. What is your team's current progress toward this goal?

7. Gather your team and begin brainstorming to assure that this goal will be completed, on time, and within budget. Reiterate your team's BOLD purpose to start this brainstorming meeting and keep their individual character strengths in mind as the brainstorming session proceeds. Each time a team member offers a solution during the brainstorming session, repeat their solution back to them, framed in the strength that's exhibited by the proposed solution (i.e., "proposing we work late demonstrates your strength of persistence").

8. From the brainstorming session, identify several potential solutions to get your team back on track to achieve the goal. Then select one of these solutions either as the team leader on behalf of your team (team leadership is not a democracy, so you can indeed choose one of the solutions), or you can involve your team in voting on the choice of a final solution.

9. Implement the solution, and agree to measure progress toward this goal at least once a week, using the agreed upon metric, and publish the results for the whole team to see each week.

10. Determine if your team's journey to goal attainment is a candidate for a team BOLD purpose reinforcement story (one told over and over to reinforce team collective spirit and BOLD purpose). If so, write a brief paragraph that encompasses the team victory.

BOLD takeaways

- As a corporate team leader or business owner, you will need to employ both evolutionary and revolutionary change strategies in order to gain a success edge over your competition.

- You can find the roadmap for evolutionary change in your company's business plan, organizational chart, and its operations manual. Revolutionary change, however, only becomes available when your team develops a "powerfully positive collective spirit" and can call upon it to go "off script" and find innovative solutions to overcome success obstacles.

- If the team can't overcome a success obstacle by following their business plan and operations procedures, then the team leader can utilize team brainstorming to conceive of innovative ideas, and potentially use one as a wedge to break through. A team that can do this has demonstrated its collective spirit and delivered effective revolutionary change. The decision to use revolutionary change is disruptive and may have significant organizational repercussions, and the decision to use it rests solely with the team leader.

- The team leader has the responsibility to develop the following five key team elements in her team: goal urgency, team BOLD purpose, clear accountability, increasing team member well-being, and entrepreneurial collaboration. A team that has these key elements present and well-developed can summon revolutionary change effectively.

- As a team leader, you can't force a team to develop a positive collective spirit, but you can and must work BOLDLY to create the conditions for this revolutionary change force to emerge when strategically needed.

Hire or fire according to strategic goals, not out of panic or convenience

It is not how much money we make that ultimately makes us happy between nine and five. It's whether our work fulfills us . . . complexity, autonomy and a relationship between effort and reward in doing creative work [are] worth more to most of us than money. . . . Hard work is a prison sentence if it does not have meaning.

— MALCOLM GLADWELL,
OUTLIERS: THE STORY OF SUCCESS

"Our airline clients need us to open three new markets for our program in 90 days, how can we do that?" asked our Sr. Product VP.

He was talking about signing up restaurants to participate in one of those airline dining club awards programs that you are probably familiar with today, where consumers use their airline charge card to eat in certain restaurants and they earn frequent flight miles. At the time, the Dining Program had just been invented by my team, and it was up to us to expand it now. The goal in each market was to get 100 restaurants signed up. This meant that we had to sign up 300 restaurants in 90 days. Not an easy task.

"Operationally, my department can handle it. It's really a sales issue and not an operational or technical issue," I chimed in as head of operations.

"There's NO WAY my sales team can sell enough participating merchants in three markets within 90 days!" our VP of Sales said, quickly throwing in the towel.

Our Sr. Product VP then turned to our outside restaurant industry consultant and asked, "What do you think we should do, Arnie?"

"I think we need to bring in Louie!" Arnie said with a slight grin.

"Who's Louie?" everyone asked, looking back and forth between each other to see if anyone knew.

We were soon to find out.

They contacted Louie and purchased his services. He promised he would spend just 30 days in each market, and walk away with a restaurant program established with 100 restaurants in each one by the deadline. A big commitment.

But Louie also drove a hard bargain; he asked for and got approval for a $10,000 per market fee—paid up front. He also negotiated for a doubling of the fee if he could get this feat accomplished in less than 90 days, even one day less. He knew our internal sales team was desperate, convinced they'd need 90 days for just one market. He knew that if they didn't capture all three markets, we would lose our largest corporate airline client who needed a restaurant base in these three cities because they were home to their largest frequent flier segments.

Nobody was sure how Louie would get this "ginormous" goal done. But our senior executives were desperate; if we could get these three cities open even one day sooner than the deadline, it would take substantial stress off them—so they agreed to Louie's deal, and sent him off to get busy.

Panic, desperation, and fear drive much of the hiring in many organizations. Anyone who was a corporate executive during the raging "dot com" years remembers the mass hysteria to hire people with any kind of internet experience. Most of those folks were fired two years later, but in 1999, even just being able to talk confidently about some brief period of internet experience was enough to land a lucrative position, and you could name your title too. Very few corporate executives had any real proficiency to call their bluff.

I also saw how hiring is too often driven by panic and fear when I owned my franchise. Many of my peer franchise business owners hired the wrong people and overpaid for them, to boot. Small business owners are a paranoid group, and they will often forgo their own fair compensation in order to overpay someone they "desperately need"—all in a misguided effort to "keep a great employee hostage to a lucrative compensation package." In other words, "Please don't leave and pursue a better job somewhere else!"

Back to Louie. The last we saw him, he walked out of our corporate offices and began actively working on opening the first of the three new markets. Our executives were excited and nervous. But something seemed strange to me. Oddly enough, when someone mentioned to one of our internal sales managers that Louie was working on the project, all he said was, "Louie!? Ha!" Apparently he was aware of this "Louie" guy.

"Do you know him?" asked our Sr. Product VP.

"Of course I know him! He'll ruin the market for everyone!" the frantic sales manager practically yelled.

"But will he get the three markets opened by himself in 90 days?" eagerly asked our pragmatic and anxious Sr. VP.

"Yes, he will, but you have no idea what he's going to do to make that happen!" responded the ever more incredulous sales manager.

The sales manager had his reasons for saying this. He knew that after Louie was done opening these markets, he'd be turning them over to the internal sales managers to manage and further develop, so any problems the new restaurant program participants had with Louie would roll downhill to them. Apparently, some of them had previously worked with Louie—and they knew his *modus operandi* and were concerned.

Looking back in hindsight, it's easy to see that our VP of Sales could have taken the "three markets in 90 days challenge" to his own internal national sales team and held a brainstorming session with them to see what innovative solutions they could propose for solving this problem. If he had held such a brainstorming session, it's highly likely his team of two dozen high-powered, smart salespeople would have come up with several potential solutions. Yes, they would have had to buy-in to the challenge, and made it their mission to get this "impossible" job done, but I believe they would have stepped up to the challenge. But the thought never even crossed the mind of our VP of Sales because he "lived by the rule book" and wasn't an inspirational leader.

Instead he chose quickly to bring in an outside "gunslinger" to take care of the problem, and then just assumed our internal sales managers would understand and accept that decision, keeping a wonderful attitude and dealing with any fall-out from the gunslinger's tactics. He didn't seem to know that when a gunslinger comes to town, people usually get hurt . . . and some even die.

So back to Louie again. The first month was ending, and Louie was sending dozens of new restaurant contracts into the home office each week. It looked like he was going to get the first market opened. The new restaurant contracts came into my department, and we processed them and prepared each restaurant for participation in our national dining program.

The second month was the same, except we heard about some crazy complaint whereby Louie was asking the restaurant owners for a bottle of expensive wine to participate in our program. This made our Sr. VP chuckle, because our internal sales team was endlessly complaining that they could not convince enough restaurants to participate—and here was Louie demanding and getting an expensive bottle of wine for the "opportunity" to participate in our program.

To almost everyone's amazement, Louie finished opening his second market in 60 days, and was now working on the third one with 30 days to go. But now Louie had a new request—he had an extra expense he needed covered and he sent it to our CFO.

"What the heck is this?" asked the CFO, handing the hand-written expense request to the Sr. VP.

"It looks like a limousine bill," said the Sr. VP.

"For $3000?!" the CFO asked incredulously.

"Well, he did get the first two markets opened, and you know how important this project is for our airline client. I think we should just consider it an investment. You know our internal sales team could never have gotten this done, so we're lucky to have Louie. Let's pay the limo bill and keep the guy focused," said our pragmatic Sr. Product VP.

Reluctantly, the CFO authorized payment to the limo service. Of course, another limousine bill for the second market, for about the same amount, came in shortly thereafter. It was also reluctantly but quickly authorized for payment.

Louie showed up at our corporate office, the week before his 90-day deadline. He had a handful of restaurant contracts in his briefcase, and handed them over to our Sr. VP.

"I got the job done early," said Louie, "so I'd like to collect my bonus now."

"Can you stay a little longer and help us make sure the new restaurants are up and running fine in our program?" asked our Sr. VP.

"No chance, I've got another consulting agreement starting next week, so I've got to run. Can I please get the bonus check while I'm here today?" Louie seemed rushed.

"Sure Louie, I'll have it for you this afternoon; why don't you get some lunch and it'll be ready when you get back."

"Sounds good," said Louie as he handed the third limousine service bill for $3,000 dollars to the Sr. VP, "Oh, and can you also please get this paid, too?"

Little did anyone know that Louie had just signed a similar deal with our direct competitor. However, it didn't matter today, as we now had 300 new restaurants signed up in three new markets. Our airline client was thrilled to hear the good news.

Louie got his bonus check, and I never saw him again. However, about a month later, we started to hear his name quite often, usually preceded by a hail of expletives. As complaints rolled in from an astounding number of restaurants in the markets Louie had opened, we were able to piece together exactly how Louie had completed his amazing feat of single-handedly opening three markets in less than 90 days.

Louie would hire a limo service for the entire month, and would schedule 15 minutes at each of the 150 largest restaurants in each town. While the limo waited outside, Louie would walk in and ask to talk to the owner. Now if you never owned a restaurant, you need to know that the owner is almost always working, so no appointment was usually needed to talk to him or her.

Louie showed the owner a blank check, with our corporate name, and a large dollar amount. He told the owner "he had 15 minutes to decide what name he wanted to see on that check. Did he want the check made out to the owner personally or to his company?"

Then Louie stood there, checking his watch, because he wasn't kidding, the owner had only 15 minutes to decide and his limo was waiting outside. As the owner tried to understand what the program he was signing up for was all about, Louie kept looking at his watch. When it ticked down, Louie gave the ultimatum—sign the contract, or the blank check would be going to the next restauranteur on the list, and he showed this list to the owner with some names already crossed off.

Most of the restaurant owners that Louie visited took the check, and many had it made it out to themselves personally—looking at it as a windfall for them. Some bought cars, others bought restaurant equipment, some paid personal bills, but none of them read the contract or understood how the program worked. Most didn't know that when our 2 million airline members dined in their restaurant in the months to come, the entire bill, including alcohol, would be drafted from the restaurant's bank account, and then up to 20% of that amount would be used to purchase airline miles, that were then added to the airline member's "frequent flyer miles balance." Louie's check was actually a discounted advance payment to the restaurant for the future dining activity and subsequent miles accumulation of the participating airline members.

During his amazing three month whirlwind limo-riding sales tour, I had the opportunity to talk to Louie for a moment (he was always in a hurry), and he told me he was a MENSA member. To this day, when I hear someone is a MENSA member, I think of you-know-who.

The keys to hiring strategically

Hiring is one of the most costly investments a company makes. Here are seven recommendations to help guide your hiring process so that you can perform it strategically and not go about hiring "Louie's" when you think you need expert help.

1. Before hiring from outside, first consider using the talent latent within your team to fill opportunities for management positions.

Businesses have constantly evolving organizations, and the role that each team member performs must also change to keep pace with the demands of a growing company and a dynamic marketplace. Having a team of people who have worked together for a year or more to solve complex client problems is a significant marketplace advantage. It makes sense to look deeper into your existing team members to determine if there is latent talent, before hiring from the outside. Hiring from your team will build the positive collective spirit of everyone else and show a connection between effort and reward.

In addition, in order to build a pipeline of potential people to promote, evaluate your organization chart and the responsibilities of each position. Wherever possible, add responsibilities for individual team members so they can grow, thrive and potentially perform beyond expectations. You'll be surprised what people can do when you give them a challenge and an opportunity to prove themselves. Seemingly ordinary people who have been working under your inspired leadership, coupled with a BOLD purpose, can achieve great things.

2. Be courageous and find creative ways to staff your team for less than was budgeted.

As you succeed, you may find yourself assigned even more important objectives for your team to take on. How can you make room for them? Your first reaction may be automatically to hire. But "busy people get busier" is a phrase used to explain the phenomenon that as your team accomplishes its objectives, they learn to handle them.

The fact is, hiring is not always the right answer to problems. It is easy to ask for ever more resources to staff your team in order to achieve the company's mission. But adopt a mindset of challenging an automatic "hiring reaction" when your team receives additional responsibilities and needs help. This will be noted by your company as an efficient use of their critical, scarce, and expensive resources. If you own the company, it also preserves some additional net profits for you.

When I owned my franchise business, I fired one highly-paid team member to make room for two new lower-paid members who could more than cover for the lost team member. This action increased our capacity to serve customers by 40 hours per week, and actually lowered my costs.

However, the resulting fall-out from this action was far more complex that I had imagined. There were unexpected consequences that I also had to accept along the way, like the fact that one of my key employees had come to heavily rely on the fired employee and was very upset by his loss—and another key employee resigned during the resulting team chaos. You'll read more about this in the chapter on BOLDskill 10.

In such times, however, you need to be courageous. I stuck to my decision, and we eventually succeeded in assimilating the two new team members and achieving our objectives while significantly lowering our costs. In the end, we became a Surging Team, and we overcame the internal and external obstacles that were preventing our successful drive to one million dollars in annual sales revenue. I just had to be brave enough to keep trying to win.

3. Use brainstorming among your team to find innovative ways to fulfill the responsibilities assigned to your team rather than hiring.

Experiment with innovation in recrafting your organization chart to try to accommodate affordable and talented people. Brainstorming is a method to encourage development of innovations through entrepreneurial collaboration among your team members, as we discussed in the prior chapter. Consider these questions as you brainstorm:

- Have any of the tasks performed by your team become obsolete and can be discontinued?

- Is there a way to automate a task that's being done manually?

- Can your client or customer perform the task for themselves using tools provided on your internet site or a smart phone application? (This is how many companies have reduced the cost of staffing their billing department—by pushing the responsibilities to their customers.)

- Is there something of value, in lieu of additional salary, that you can offer a key staff member who agrees to attempt difficult goals?

It was during one of these brainstorming sessions with my internal team and a few trusted advisors that I realized our dining rewards program did not require subscribers to carry a specific "discount card"—but could instead use any credit card in their wallet to trigger their reward automatically. This revelation not only launched our new product, but it eventually influenced the entire "credit card rewards" industry.

4. Be sure that someone is cross-trained to cover each critical task.

Don't hire one person with special expertise and believe that the game is done. You also must make sure that you have other people on your team who know how to do most of what this specialist can do.

When I had my franchise business, our owner peer-collaboration group was in the midst of critiquing the business performance of one of our colleagues, Gary. We asked him, "Why are you paying Dan, your senior staff member, a six-figure salary, while paying yourself so little as the owner and president?"

The answer was distressing and revealed that a counter-productive employment policy was in place, "Dan said that if he didn't get paid at least six figures, he'd have to find another job. If Dan quits, I'll lose my clients. He's the only one who knows what we do for them."

If you're leading a corporate team, or own the company, you need to assure that others on the team (or at least that you personally) are cross-trained to perform each critical service task. The cross-trained team members may not perform the task as efficiently as the expert, but if you have only one person on the team capable of performing a task, you open yourself up to a serious risk and failure of team leadership that you can't afford. If you don't have other staff members who have the skills to learn these critical tasks, then consider replacing a team member to bring in this skill. It's difficult to let people go, especially people who've been loyal employees, but your team depends on you to assure that they have the appropriate depth of skills within the group.

You also can't control when a critical team member leaves or is temporarily unable to function in their role. So if you don't have a plan to manage each critical task in the absence of a key team member, then you increase the risk that your team will fail. This is the most often cited reason for the failure of a company or a team—the loss of a key member at an inopportune time—and the lack of an effective plan to replace the lost skill set. You must have a plan in place that responds quickly to the loss of any team member and assures that your team can recover quickly and get back to achieving its goals, on time and within budget.

5. Use a company-approved, work-focused, personality test and don't discount the results. In fact, multiply any annoying, odd, and otherwise "slightly crazy" behavior observed during an interview by a factor of 10.

If your business employs even one person besides you or your spouse, you have to protect yourself, your team, and your company from any individual staff member losing their mind on any given day. There may be pressure to quickly hire someone who has the skill set you need, which causes you to overlook telltale clues about future problems and become overly confident in their ability to successfully contribute to your team. A good rule of thumb I use is to multiply anything a job candidate does or says that bothers you in an interview by a factor of ten. Literally!

For example, if somebody mentions "parties" in a job interview, or shows up wearing disheveled clothing, it's likely that person has personal problems, and you don't need that drama in your company.

Now we are all human, so most potential employees have some personal problems, of course. You'll still need to hire some of them, but I recommend that you use a standardized personality test focused on employment success (like the one offered by CRI at criw.com). But if you do this, be prepared to accept, believe and act on what the test results show. Do not feel timid or guilty and hire a person whose test results leave you scratching your head. Here's what can happen when you don't listen to the personality test results.

"I think I'm having an allergic reaction to shell fish," exclaimed my new hire.

It was the first day at my company for two new hires. I invited both out to lunch, along with our Service Delivery Manager. We went to a Japanese steak house, and we all ordered steak. As we waited for our meal to arrive, we drank green tea and I explained my expectations for my team. I passed around a copy of my infamous "Consider Carefully the Challenge" email from a few years ago, where I challenged my staff members to either gird themselves for the extreme challenges of growing our company, or submit their resignation letter now. After reading the email aloud at our table, that's when one of the two new hires stood up suddenly and exclaimed that "he was having an allergic reaction to shellfish."

"But we're not eating shellfish," I said in bewilderment, as the fellow paced around, waving his hand in front of his face.

"Our silverware or glassware must have touched shellfish," he retorted.

"Why don't you go outside and get some fresh air?" I suggested.

The new hire went outside, and returned quickly to rejoin the conversation, but within a few minutes he was back on his feet pacing, and waving his hand in front of his face.

"Have you ever had a shellfish reaction before?" I asked.

"No," he said.

"Then how would you know it's a shellfish allergic reaction?" I queried.

"I need you to take me to the emergency care center right now!" he replied.

"OK, there's one just a couple of blocks away, let's go," I said, responding to his increasingly urgent behavior.

We went to emergency care, and I took him back to his car a couple of hours later, after he was released.

As I thought about the incident, I recalled his personality test results reading that "this candidate is under *severe* stress." After I read that in his test results, I'd projected my own imagined reason for his *severe* stress, thinking it was obviously because he was unemployed and facing financial pressure. So I let it go and hired him. But now, I was almost certain that he had an anxiety attack on his first day at work, and I had two other witnesses. When I asked the other staff who had come to lunch, they agreed it was definitely an anxiety attack.

There was no way this new employee could perform the job responsibilities I would need him to do, so I decided to fire him the next day. I paid him for a full week (although he only worked ½ day) out of courtesy. I met him in the morning to deliver the bad news. He didn't argue, but his wife called me later threatening to sue and claiming discrimination (against who? shellfish allergy sufferers?), but I ignored the threat and never heard from either of them again. They did cash my check.

From that point, I vowed to pay close attention when a new hire's personality test identifies that the person is under "severe stress." It's a sure sign of potential drama or craziness at a future date.

6. Don't overpay for talent, and do reward your team members
   for achievement of team objectives.

Some owners and team leaders develop an "imposter syndrome," in which they feel that they're not qualified to perform the group governance roles, especially when their service relies on specialized expertise they don't personally have. Others believe that owning a business or leading a high profile corporate team gives them the license to delegate all the group governance role work. In both cases, this often results in grossly overpaying for talent or hiring additional and costly staff to compensate for what they cannot do.

If you are a team leader, overpaying is a sure way to flag you as fungible, ineffective, and expendable. You may feel inadequately prepared to perform the group governance roles, but anyone can overpay to compensate for this feeling. Your team will notice when you've over-compensated in a hiring decision, and you will lose credibility and trust. It's better to struggle with learning new skills than to give up and hire someone to do your job.

If you are the owner, overpaying someone to perform roles you're not comfortable performing will only result in near-zero net profits, near-zero owners' compensation, and potentially the loss of your business one day when that person quits and your clients see him (and he sees himself) as the real owner anyway.

On the other hand, hiring people who were previously making far more in their previous job is equally risky, and you need to pay close attention to the results of what should be a mandatory personality test of all new employees. Lingering feelings of resentment (if they accept a lower compensation) are poison for your company.

As a wise philosopher and country music singer, Billy Currington, once said, "God is great, beer is good, and people are crazy." People are all slightly crazy, but you need to hire some of them. The team or company that can best assemble a team of ordinary people, inspire them to great performance while keeping costs down, can transform ordinary teams into unstoppable Surging Teams. Those are the firms that will win in the marketplace.

Your role as the owner or team leader is to provide a way to make your critical team members feel like they own the company's mission—and act like owners, all while understanding and accepting their role as employees. It's up to you to make sure they understand and respect that you deserve to be paid fairly for your leadership role. They should also understand that you can't and won't overpay for your employees and team members.

Negotiate for ways to pay a bonus if team objectives are met which result in additional net profits for the company. This is the way to increase ownership behavior and encourage attainment of team objectives.

7. Don't hire out of panic, desperation, or convenience.

Panic and convenience hiring is a sure way to get a temporary gunslinger who leaves a wake of chaos which can easily ruin a Surging Team. Remember Louie!

It's worth it to be prepared when it comes to hiring by having a pipeline of candidates at the ready. I used to place ads in the local paper and interview people, even when we weren't hiring—just to keep a short list of pre-qualified, potential team members. This allowed us to shorten the hiring cycle by 4-6 weeks when I did need to hire someone new or replace someone, and avoid a hiring emergency. It was a kind of insurance policy to have some "already interviewed candidates" ready to step forward when needed.

You can use the Strategic Hiring Worksheet provided in Appendix K to help analyze your hiring practices.

AN INTERESTING TWIST ON HIRING

If you have the opportunity as a small business owner or team leader to hire someone, try to find someone who is open to the idea of one day buying you out. You can screen for this "eventual buy-out vision" during the hiring process. Some people don't want to consider owning their own company, but more and more people are being forced to consider this scenario, out of necessity, as a way to achieve higher incomes—the "necessity entrepreneurs." People who express an openness to one-day "owning their own business" may find it attractive to accept a position for "less than marketplace compensation" if they believe you are giving them a unique career opportunity in future years.

Most people don't have the capital to start a business outright, but they would be able to help you build your company—and then buy you out in a structured buy-out scenario. Having a "one day I'll own this company" mindset makes a huge difference in the ownership engagement people feel as they perform their work and how they respond to challenges and work stress. They can get very creative and innovative, and their persistence is measurably more sustained that the typical employee who is simply working for wages.

Firing someone is tough, but sometimes it must be done

If you follow our BOLDskills methodology, and create a Surging Team, you will reduce turnover on your team, but you can never eliminate the need to occasionally fire someone in order to protect your team's ability to always succeed. No team leader enjoys firing someone, especially someone whom he has also hired. It makes you question your own judgment, since you hired the person. But, as team leader, you must take this responsibility seriously. Firing someone is a far more vital and potentially risky leadership task than you may imagine. Here are 7 tips I have learned about why, when, and how to fire someone.

1. Don't allow your team to suffer from negativity or incompetence introduced by one member.

I knew it was going to be bad. Our new stock broker client was unable to perform trades earlier this week because his computer network firewall wasn't operating properly when the trading window opened at 6 a.m. on Monday. Our senior service technician, Rick, only a few months on our team, had been assigned to this client. The owner called me into a meeting first thing the following day. I was ushered into a conference room and sat there with some other fellow I didn't know. We said hello, but didn't introduce ourselves. The owner finally came in and sat down. He looked over at me.

"You're fired," he said to me, "Over here is our former service company owner and he'll need a few minutes with you to do a service turnover back to his company." With that, the owner got up and left.

The old, and now suddenly-new-again service company owner looked at me with a smug smile. I was too shell-shocked to be nervous, so I just said, "Remember, you got fired before I did."

That wiped the smugness off his face, and we finished a quick turnover meeting and I went outside to find that the sun was still shining.

This incident of our company being fired by this stock broker client led to my meeting the following day with our senior service technician, Rick. There had been prior warning signs that I overlooked, but now I knew I had to terminate him for causing the loss of this client by an obvious and careless "rookie" oversight—not testing for internet access after replacing network equipment.

"Please, you can't do this to me," pleaded Rick.

I had booked a public place for this meeting in a library because I didn't want a scene, and if there was a scene, I wanted witnesses.

"I'm sorry Rick, but as of now, you're no longer working for our company. If you sign this agreement to cease communication with our clients immediately, and if you return our equipment, then you'll receive two weeks of severance pay.

Rick looked at me with a sad glance and again pleaded. I was very sorry to have to tell him the news, but it had been my decision to hire him and now my decision to fire him. When he was hired, I thought he was a confident and independent worker—and he seemed to be just what we needed. It turns out that Rick was indeed confident and independent, but he wasn't competent and his customer service skills were poor—a problem for a senior computer technician. This was fully on display when our new stock brokerage client, whom Rick had been assigned to, was unable to access the internet or execute a stock trade earlier this week, which justifiably got us fired. Rick was not a fit for us, so after just three months of work, I let him go and found a replacement with the skills that our clients needed and deserved.

Rick slowly pulled the paperwork toward him, read it over, signed it, and then got up to leave. I thought of saying something, but I held back and just sat at the table and watched him leave. There wasn't anything else I could say and nothing he could do would save the situation. He had to just move on and honor our agreement.

Here's another example of how I had to fire an employee who introduced negativity onto our team. This situation began when I heard that Fred, a new service technician I had hired who was a recent college graduate, had been discussing salaries with my other staff members.

"Fred, did you really tell the other team members that you were unhappy with your salary, in your first week of working here?" I asked him.

"Well, yes," said Fred.

"Then you're fired," I said.

"Don't I get another chance?!" Fred pleaded.

"Not here, but maybe at your next job you'll work for a few months before you start asking about salary increases—and discuss it directly with the boss and not your co-workers."

I bet Fred didn't complain about his compensation for a good, long while after his one-week job experience at my company.

2. Be on the lookout for people who have quit, but failed to tell you.

While I was a corporate executive and pursuing an MBA program in the evenings, this topic was a major eye-opener for me:

"When do employees quit?" asked our professor.

The obvious answer from our class of competitive students was shouted out, "If they're offered a higher salary or a better opportunity by another company!"

"Those are good reasons to quit, but it's not what I asked," said the professor. "*When* do employees quit?"

People were puzzled, so he finally relinquished the answer: "An employee actually quits when in their mind they begin to seriously think and fantasize about quitting. This usually happens well before—sometimes even years before—announcing that they quit, and usually before receiving another job offer."

What I gleaned from this lesson was powerful. As promoted by psychologists for decades, self-talk is powerful. Self-talk allows you imagine yourself in another situation. In doing so, you have a powerful jumpstart to actually change your current circumstances to achieve that imagined situation. This is what happens when people think about quitting. Once somebody decides it in their mind, they may stay with you for weeks, months, or years—but mentally they've already imagined a new situation for themselves outside of your company. They will finally choose to leave just as soon as they have the opportunity. You can't save them. You can't pay them enough. You'll know who they are because eventually the change in their performance and attitude will out them. They may even become "bad apples or sour grapes" on your team.

Rather than trying to rehabilitate these people, you're better off identifying who has "mentally quit," firing them, and finding another team member who wants the job badly and will come with a great attitude. Learn to do it quickly, and increase your chances of business success. Spending time and money trying to "save them" is . . . well, it's crazy.

If you know someone has mentally quit, and let them stay by rationalizing their behavior, you get situations like the following.

"I'm so upset with your company right now that I'm not sure we can continue one more day with your service!" It was a Sunday morning, and I was getting ready for our family's church service. This call to my personal cell phone blindsided me.

Recognizing the voice of one of our clients, I asked, "Karen, what's the matter?"

"Your service technician sent a text to our boss this morning, asking if he was 'finally done whining now'."

I was confused. Then I saw the text sent by our service technician to a "texting group" that included our client's owner. It was a stupid mistake made by our less-than-happy service technician who was trying to help a difficult client on the weekend. But now, what was intended as above-and-beyond weekend assistance by my service team member turned into a devastating client-relationship nightmare. The sarcasm that was meant only for our internal staff was irretrievably texted to our client.

My heart sank and the future revenues from this long-time client flashed before my eyes. Embarrassment is too mild a word; I felt physically ill. I doubted the client would ever forgot this slight, and so I had to present myself at his office first thing on Monday, apologizing and asking for forgiveness and another chance.

In the end, we didn't lose the client, and I settled for a private reprimand of this employee and didn't fire her for this mistake—but I should have. This employee had already mentally quit.

We did make it to our church service and found many other things to be thankful for!

3. Don't rationalize like this: "I really need to keep [insert the name of a "can't-do-without-employee.] What if I just paid him more to stay?"

There are several problems with this thinking. The first is that people rarely tell you the actual reason they're leaving or thinking about leaving. Instead, they'll give you the reason they think best fits the circumstance to make them look better. The second reason is that you have a fiduciary responsibility to keep your costs in line with the marketplace, especially in the critical area of salaries, because if you don't, you put your entire company at risk. The third reason is one that you may not be aware of, but it comes as a result of the first reason. The fact is that even if you paid your staff member more to try to keep them, they are going to leave your company anyway. It's almost always true, and it's because they didn't tell you the real reason that they wanted to leave in the first place. They may not even know the underlying reason themselves, but they constantly imagine themselves NOT working for you or your company.

Do not underestimate the overwhelming weight and the gravitational pull of wages and compensation on your company's financial success, as they are usually the largest expense items in your business. Some of the top business owners in my former franchise system were given wise staffing and compensation advice by their peers, but were unable to accept the task of initiating stressful conversations with their staff to keep wages in line. They preferred to "not rock the boat," and a few of them had the boat capsize on them as it sank.

4. Don't believe: "I need each of my team members and can't let anyone go."

Our franchise business owner peer-collaboration group had zeroed in on the obviously high team compensation burden that one of our colleagues was carrying. We knew that she had too many employees and that her company could not afford to have such a high employee compensation burden.

"Your organization chart shows that you're carrying too many people. Their compensation can't be supported by your revenues and profit margin. You're losing money month over month" we reasoned with her.

"It's not possible to do it without them; I need each of those positions!" insisted our peer.

"But you can do some of those tasks yourself," we coaxed.

"I don't like to do those tasks. If I do those tasks, I can't focus on what I like to do. I should be able to do what I like to do and what I'm good at doing. What's the point of being the owner if I don't have the freedom to work on what I like to do?"

Then it became clear. Our colleague felt entitled to do whatever tasks made her happiest—and not necessarily the strategic tasks that an owner must perform—especially those that result in financial success—like assuring intentional development of the group governance roles of: ownership engagement, inspired leadership, and trusted management.

If you're leading a corporate team, you may be similarly asked to reduce your payroll in response to a budget crunch. How will you respond? Early in my corporate career, when I was asked to reduce payroll, I resisted and passionately argued a case for keeping each team member. But this behavior only got me branded as an immature leader and possibly an obstructionist. Later in my corporate career, I was finally able to view requests to reduce staff as an opportunity to act like a business owner, appropriately matching expenditures to budgets. Being asked to reduce payroll was a great chance to reimagine departmental functions. It's so easy to just keep hiring another person, but being asked to reimagine your team's staffing and individual objectives is an opportunity to conceive of innovative solutions. You may be able to eliminate redundant procedures, redistribute tasks, or redesign job descriptions to spread responsibility wider and deeper across the remaining team members.

Believe your financial projections and follow your business plan. Firing one person to save everyone else's job, or even save your company, is the right thing to do if your expected revenues can't support your current staffing level.

You may also find that as your company grows, you need staff with different talents in order to catapult the team to the next level. You likely can't afford both all the original team members as well as hire new folks with the talents you now find your company needs. Yes, you'll be faced with firing someone who hasn't done anything wrong, but doesn't have to talent to help your team achieve its ultimate objectives. But you need to make room for critical talent, and so you must summon your courage to manage your team to success.

5. Don't think you can "ride out" a revenue shortfall or carry a non-performing team member.

At a time when it would be most prudent to fire someone, you may decide to try to "ride-out" a revenue shortfall or carry a non-performing or fungible team member. Some companies even proclaim that this is one of their strengths, that they don't fire people when they feel economic and financial pressure. This may be possible to do without severe consequences if you are leading a large company, one that can sustain operating below the breakeven or efficiency point with a reasonable expectation that the revenues will eventually rise to cover the cost of the "carried staff." But this is usually not possible among small firms and entrepreneurial start-ups or franchise locations.

Shedding team members to reduce compensation costs is a constant option for staying within budget. If you can't fire people to keep your company solvent, or keep the right skills on your team, then you likely don't have the fortitude to make the frequent, difficult decisions that a leader and manager must make in order to achieve their team's objectives.

Taking no action in the face of an obvious company financial challenge, or an obvious skills shortfall or employee problem is, in fact, making a decision. Not to decide is to decide. But not deciding is less than bold; it is a bad choice that will delay efficient company performance and potentially sink your business.

If you find that you have to fire someone to keep your costs down "for a season," then use the opportunity to evaluate the job marketplace with an eye toward hiring cheaper labor and lowering your costs in order to compete even more effectively. It's your fiduciary responsibility as the owner and team leader to keep your costs in line with the industry, and as low as reasonably possible, in order to still achieve your team's objectives. This will increase your company's valuation.

6. Fire quickly.

Beware: your employees and team members may try to sabotage your business either intentionally or unintentionally, even though you're paying them well, treating them kindly, and otherwise trying to help them. I've seen three instances of inside sabotage, including embezzlement and fraud. You as the team leader need to ensure that you are not overlooking clues to poor performance or criminal behavior that will sink your team. People need to be held accountable for their work and there must be metrics in place to help identify inconsistencies and hold your team members responsible for how they behave at work.

Allowing a failing employee to continue to work for you beyond the point that you realize they are failing or doing petty criminal actions harms a Surging Team. By the time you realize they're failing, your other team members and your clients have already figured this out, and they're watching to see how you'll handle it. Do it quickly, do it yourself, do it in person, and do it in a public place. Also, don't negotiate while firing someone—just be fair to them with a severance package, but fire them and then walk away. To do otherwise is not fully accepting your role as manager, and you'll lose trust.

Beware of this trap: Difficult management decisions will take all the time that you set aside for them. For instance, if you tell yourself that you'll "take the weekend" to decide on something, then you will tend to make the decision either before you go to bed on Sunday night, or even "just minutes before 8 a.m." Monday morning. Your staff needs strong and confident management, and your decision making process needs to be short. Instead of "taking the entire weekend" to think over things, set yourself a clear time that is no more than one day away. For instance, I used to make a commitment to make my critical "hire or fire" decisions on Saturday mornings by 11 a.m. That gave me the rest of the weekend to envision how I was going to implement my decision, and to get comfortable with it.

When it comes to firing someone, do it as soon as you start feeling they need to leave your company. If you "wait for them to quit," they can do tremendous damage before they do, and you've just abdicated your power to them.

7. After you fire a staff member, meet with your team individually.

You want to ensure that you are maintaining the trust of each of your remaining team members and maybe even some important clients by quickly meeting one-on-one with each of them. Let them know that your lost staff member is no longer working for your company, but that your team is well-equipped and motivated to continue and deliver its promised services. This will reaffirm your role as the team leader and maintain your Surging Team. In doing this, you may manage to save each remaining team member and all client relationships, but on the other hand, you may not, since some of your clients may equate your company's service with the now-fired staff member. However, your quick and decisive personal action will give you the best outcome.

You can use the Strategic Firing Worksheet included in Appendix L to analyze your current firing practices.

SHOW STRENGTH WHEN TERMINATED EMPLOYEES MISBEHAVE

If you learn that a terminated employee has begun to contact your clients directly, you may feel powerless to stop them and unable to spend the time or the energy to demand that they respect the confidentiality and non-compete employment agreements you have in place with them. You may think, "I've already fired them, what can I do? Yes, my staff member signed a non-compete, but by the time I fight this injustice, it will be too late to recover—and apparently my clients were ok with this because they agreed to a new service arrangement directly with my former staff member."

This response is weak and indecisive. You need to assure that your team knows that you will not tolerate it and will fight hard against unfairness, unethical, or criminal behavior. Consult a lawyer, and at minimum have her send a stern letter reminding the former staff member about their employment agreement with your company and possible legal action if they ignore it. Do not become inert and let terminated employees clean you out.

BOLD takeaways

- Panic and convenience hiring is a sure way to get a temporary gunslinger who leaves a wake of chaos which can easily ruin a Surging Team. It's also a good way to overpay an employee and cause you and your company financial strain. Remember Louie!

- Use a personality test to screen job applicants, then be sure to believe what the results tell you before you extend a job offer and hire someone who's "really crazy."

- To keep your Surging Team together as long as possible, evaluate your organization chart and the responsibilities of each position. Wherever possible, add responsibilities for individual team members to grow, thrive, and potentially perform beyond expectations. Use team brainstorming to find ways to distribute new tasks instead of hiring someone new. When you do need to hire, try to promote existing staff. Sometimes we get too familiar with people performing in their existing roles and can't imagine them in a new position with more responsibility. You'll be surprised what people can do when you give them an opportunity, and it increases the team's collective spirit to hire from within.

- Consciously work to keep your staffing costs down. This is usually a company's largest expense item and it is the easiest to lose control over. Overpaying for employees is an ineffective way to try to stop team turnover, but usually only attracts underperformers. It also increases the company's financial burden and unnecessarily reduces company profits. Find other ways to compensate valued team members than merely higher salaries.

- Do you have a rating for how each member of your team is performing today? Are each of your team members meeting or exceeding your expectations? If they're not meeting expectations, then why are they still working for your team?

- Keep an eye out for team members who quit, but "fail to tell you." When you identify one, make it a formal separation. Someone who has mentally quit will almost never be able to be "talked or compensated back into being a productive and happy team member." They will keep imagining themselves NOT working for your team. Trust me on this and save yourself the heartache of learning it for yourself. When you do determine that you need to fire someone, do it quickly and don't drag the decision out and endlessly debate it.

- Be sure to have someone else, even if it's you, familiar with each task that the team performs. Be prepared for the day when someone quits. Never put your team into a situation where someone can leave your company and render the remaining staff helpless.

Practice win-win negotiation in all spheres of your business relationships

So much of life is a negotiation—so even if you're not in business, you have opportunities to practice all around you.
— KEVIN O'LEARY, CO-HOST OF ABC'S "SHARK TANK"

Our industry consultant and "gunslinger," Arnie, listened patiently to me. I explained that a bank vice president was refusing to cooperate and send us restaurant credit card transactions that would allow us to identify our customers' dining program activity.

"I tried everything, and there's no way this guy's going to agree to send us credit card transactions from his bank," I lamented. "I spoke to him three times already, and he won't budge."

For other large merchant banks, I'd been able to use the name-dropping specter of our corporate parent to get them to send us their credit card transactions from our participating restaurant partners, since we needed to see the transactions to credit bonus miles for the airline's customers. This allowed us to identify when our participating airline members dined in participating restaurants, by finding and matching their card numbers. But I could not get past this particular executive at a key merchant bank—one used by many of our participating restaurants. Without the transactions, those restaurants would not be able to join our program.

"Give me his phone number," Arnie said calmly. Without hesitation, he dialed the number and the merchant bank executive answered. I only heard Arnie's side of the conversation.

"I know you already talked to my colleague, Scott Brennan, about an agreement between our company and your bank," Arnie began. There was some response by the bank executive.

"Listen, we have 10,000 participating restaurants in our national dining program. If we can't come to some agreement with you, we'll have to recommend that our restaurants use another merchant bank for their credit card payments. Your bonus depends on coming to a mutually beneficial agreement with us," Arnie reasoned. "We'll make it worth your while," he winked at me with a twinkling eye.

There was a pause.

"Ok, we can do that," said Arnie, "Send over your contract revisions this afternoon and we'll get it signed," and he ended the call.

I was shocked at Arnie's boldness and the quick turnaround by the merchant bank's executive. When I asked Arnie how he managed to get it done—he simply said, "He just had to know what was in it for him, and then have a way to 'save face.'"

I had been expecting that Arnie would demand that this executive work with us, and if he refused, then we'd threaten to engage "at a higher corporate level." Instead, Arnie negotiated it as a win-win. His tactic was basically, "You can change a few minor terms in the contract, and keep your restaurant clients, along with some reasonable compensation to your company for helping us; and you keep your executive bonus. In exchange, we get our credit card stream. Win-win deal done.

Everyone hates losing, so recognize opportunities and always negotiate win-win deals

As the above story relates, everyone hates losing and will fight tooth and nail if they believe they'll end up getting a bad deal and losing. Sometimes you need to step back, pretend you're the other party, and imagine what they want in the deal. That's what Arnie did in the above story.

Most of us have experienced a negotiation that left us feeling the dreaded "buyers' remorse," an unsettling awareness that someone tricked or bullied us into an unfair agreement. The sooner you realize that almost all the important decisions you face as an entrepreneur or business leader are really opportunities for a win-win negotiation, and you agree in your mind to help the other person in the negotiation get what they need—the more likely you are to succeed in your business. If the other party to the negotiation feels like they're "losing," they will either exit the negotiation up front, or they'll attempt to sabotage it later.

Achieving mastery at win-win negotiating takes practice, but it's a skill that will save you money, help you and your team achieve your goals, and is a powerful strategic tool to use as the leader of your Surging Team to keep your group on track. But in order to use it effectively, you've got to practice it. That's why it's one of the BOLDskills.

Learning how to identify a win-win opportunity is part of that practice. Most contracts present you with a win-win opportunity, as do many of your interactions with others who have resources that you need—even if it's not a formal agreement you're looking for. But as with your opportunity awareness, you need to have the presence of mind to recognize win-win negotiating opportunities, and then have the courage to pursue a negotiation.

Below, I provide you with some examples of win-win negotiating from my experience as a corporate executive and as a company owner where I was able to recognize a negotiating opportunity, and then leverage win-win negotiation—even though it wasn't a typical contractual scenario.

THE SOURCES OF POWER IN A NEGOTIATION

a. *Positional power.* This person is always the boss or the bigger fish.

b. *Expert power.* This person holds specialized knowledge as a form of power.

c. *Charismatic power.* This person has power to affect others, which can't be duplicated as it is largely intuitive and inherited.

d. *Coercive power.* This person is all about win-lose negotiation.

e. *Persuasive power.* This person utilizes win-win negotiation, a skill that can be learned and repeated.

f. *Reward power.* This person uses rewards to entice others to give in.

The best negotiating position is to be someone who has Persuasive power combined with either Positional or Expert power.

Win-win negotiation with internal company teams

Win-win negotiation directly pertains to intrapreneurs leading an internal team who must creatively achieve results for their employer. Sometimes this negotiation involves external parties, like the bank executive in the story above. Other times the negotiation involves your own internal departments and their valuable resources.

If you're leading a corporate unit, for example, you may believe that the company's resources are all there to automatically help you. That is far from the actual case. There are more demands on the company's operational resources—telemarketing call center, mail room, data entry people, customer service department, as well as the company's professional resources such as attorneys, actuaries, human resources, computer programming, accounting—than they can possibly handle. These internal departments are constantly prioritizing, and it's up to you as the leader of your corporate unit to become a good win-win negotiator.

For example, when I was working for GE in the dining rewards program division, there were many times that I had to engage our corporate attorney. The problem was, unbelievably, he would often doze off in the midst of our conversation. So I took matters into my own hands, and started to bring him drafts of the contracts I wanted to initiate—like one we needed to execute *today* with a merchant bank that handled credit card transactions. My draft got our corporate attorney's attention, and circumvented a long and painful "contract drafting process" with our internal legal team. Our attorney got less sleep, but I was able to get a new contract approved in a day or two, after he added *"force majeure"* and a few other important legalese clauses to my draft. If you think these drafts were unwise because I am not an attorney, you need to know that when GE sold my division, 100% of these contracts with merchant banks transitioned successfully to the new owner.

I was constantly practicing win-win negotiation with our internal legal team. They appreciated that I'd been proactive and created a contract draft that included most of the business and technical components of the agreement. This allowed me to get many new contracts approved quickly and continue to drive our product team's snow-balling success. If I would have simply "demanded faster contract review & approval turnaround," or tried to escalate my contract requests to the senior executive ranks—I would have been branded "insubordinate" and we would have failed in our team mission.

Here is another example of negotiating for the resources of a critical internal department.

"Come in Scott, I've got some great news," our Senior VP invited me into his office.

"Hi Troy, what's up?" I asked curiously.

"Our airline partners loved the new dining program, and they want us to market it to their two million elite frequent flier members in Q1. You and your team have done a fantastic job bringing this new service to market, so congratulations on your promotion to Assistant Vice President."

Troy waited for me to react to my promotion news. I smiled and thanked him, but my mind raced ahead to a huge problem we now faced—our computer systems were designed as a working prototype, and would soon crash and burn under a national roll-out to two million airline members.

"Thanks Troy, I appreciate that. We're going to need extra support from the IT team to make this happen," I floated the problem out there to see how Troy reacted, but he was ecstatic about the airline marketing partnership, and was unfazed.

"Sure, Scott, no problem, you go ahead and work something out with IT. Congratulations again." Troy reached out and shook my hand and escorted me out the door.

I thought of how I could negotiate something with my peer, Don, the Assistant VP of IT, to secure the computer resources we needed. If we could come to an agreement and then jointly present it to his boss, the VP of IT, then we'd have a chance. I peeked into Don's office.

"Hi Don, do you have a minute?" Don was always busy, but he put down his work and waved me in.

"Sure, what's on your mind, Scott?" Like me, Don wasn't much for small talk.

"We've got a problem, Don. Marketing just announced a national rollout of our program to two million airline frequent fliers in Q1, and our system prototype can't handle that volume. We need to bring it in-house, and fast." I tried my best to make it our shared problem.

"That is a problem, Scott. Our Q1 project calendar for IT is completely full, there's no way we can get that done."

Don wasn't kidding. I was already very familiar with the perennial issue of "far too many IT projects and far too little time or professional staff," but I had come prepared with a win-win.

"I'd like to propose a solution. Are you open to hearing it?" I wanted Don's buy-in at each step.

"Sure, let's hear it, but it better be really good," Don smiled in a way that communicated to me that he didn't think there was anything that could change the Q1 IT calendar.

"Marketing is willing to pay for database and programming language training for your entire computer programming team. You choose the database, you choose the computer language, and you can even choose the training company. All we ask is that your team uses these skills to build a new production system for our dining product by the end of Q1." I paused and waited for Don's response.

Don's countenance changed as he considered this windfall offer. Having worked on the IT staff, I knew that the height of job satisfaction in their profession was to be trained in a new programming language or database, and then be asked to use these skills and tools to develop a new production system. Maintaining old computer systems was tough work, not fun at all, and it was 95% of what Don's IT staff was currently assigned to. This offer would boost morale in his department for years.

"Hmmm . . . I have to admit, that's a heck of an offer. Are you sure you can get that cost approved? We don't have budget for that in IT," Don leaned forward now and his smile turned serious.

"It's already approved, you just need to agree to the Q1 timeframe and get to work picking your programming language, database, and training consultants," I optimistically promised.

"Can you put that in writing for me so we can get the ball rolling? I think I can sell that to Bill." Don looked genuinely excited now.

"Done, I'll get you the approval letter by the end of the day," I committed. Heck, I was not about to wait for another lesson on "how to act like a director" from Sr. VP Jane.

The above win-win negotiation was approved by senior management, and our in-house computer system was successfully developed by a highly motivated programming team in our IT department. Everybody won in that negotiation, and then went on winning in their careers for years as a result.

Win-win negotiating with vendor partners

Your vendor partnerships are an external extension of your team. If you continue to negotiate with your vendors, and recognize that the agreement between you must always be a win-win, then your team will be able to count on your vendors any time they need them.

Letting a long-ago negotiated agreement with a vendor remain in place without regularly reviewing it for win-win potential is also a missed opportunity. Old agreements will quickly atrophy from neglect, and tilt in favor of either you or the vendor, becoming a win-lose. Here's an example of how important it is for a Surging Team to have a win-win agreement in place with a trusted vendor:

"How many people signed up for our credit card?" asked our credit card processing vendor.

"23," I replied, clearly dejected at the embarrassingly low number.

The marketing test-offer for our dining program had been elaborate and expensive. We'd even flown our corporate jet to the launch event, and the 23 credit card applications didn't even pay for the in-flight peanuts. The "call to action" in our promotion was for the recipient of our offer to sign up for our privately-issued "Dining Credit Card." We knew we could track the transactions from this credit card since it was issued by our merchant bank, who was also our credit card processing vendor. By tracking the transactions, we'd know when a cardholder had visited one of the restaurants in our program—and we could then issue a dining discount to the cardholder. But only 23 people responded to our marketing test, and so it seemed to be a spectacular failure. As we looked over these miserable results, our vendor recognized something that would change everything.

"Well, we did prove that we could track credit card transactions," said the vendor. Then we both looked at each other and it seemed we had the same idea.

"We don't need to issue our own private credit card in order to track the transactions, do we!" I said. This wasn't a question; it was a realization and an observation. We both smiled at the recognition that ANY credit card currently possessed by our customers could be tracked by sifting through the restaurant's credit card transactions—it didn't have to be the privately-issued credit card that we had created ourselves. After all, nearly everybody already had a credit card from some bank, including all the two million elite frequent flier customers of our major airline partner.

Working with the vendor in this way proved the power of our win-win relationship. We had treated this vendor as an extension of our team, and we had a win-win relationship in place. Today, it paid off in a big way as the vendor helped my team identify a huge marketplace opportunity that transformed a failed marketing test into a huge advantage. If our vendor search had been simply based on finding a vendor with the lowest price for their service, we may never have found the great collaborative relationship that exposed our big idea—the one that would soon allow us to explode our dining program into the market.

As a side note, I'm not advocating that you don't negotiate to keep your costs down with your vendors. It's always a good exercise to review alternatives to current vendor partners, and let them know this is your policy. They will be extra cautious about raising their rates or reducing their service level with you and you'll earn their continued respect. But in the end, you don't want to be looking for the cheapest vendor, but rather the vendor who offers your team the best value—which also includes their talent and creative contributions to your team.

Win-win negotiating with clients and customers through your service contract

If your business uses service contracts, they are a great negotiation opportunity to find new clients if you approach it from a win-win position. One of the ways that I would do this is simplify them to the point of making signing our service contract a no-brainer. Why use a 9-page service agreement, when a 1-page agreement is all that's needed? Don't make your service agreement so onerous that it interferes with explaining what service was purchased, the costs, and clear language on how both parties will proceed. Leave off the threats and nasty language.

The biggest risk for my franchise business was not having enough clients, so I didn't want to unnecessarily scare any away. I knew that if I had opportunities to present our services one-on-one to potential clients, that I could explain our value, win some sales, and then provide the kind of service that would compel my clients to want to continue and pay for. Poor service would not compel a client to pay me for very long.

Of course, your attorney will likely recommend a very "tight and lengthy service contract," which contains all the protections you need for a binding agreement, while earning him big fees. But what if your client decides not to pay you regardless of the agreed upon terms? Ask yourself: Am I really going to sue a client if they break the service agreement? If the answer is yes, then you should use the 9–page agreement. If the answer is no, then a single page may be all that's needed. A single page was all that my company needed when I ran my franchise business. I believed that my company was far better off if I used my time meeting with and winning more clients—than spending time in court to force compliance. Besides, I figured that if and when we did experience client service disputes, we'd negotiate a win-win resolution in most cases, save a good client, and never even consider going to court.

Clients love to negotiate with a small business owner and they will do so regardless of the contract they initially signed—at every opportunity they have. They read the same books you do and have the same vested interest in their own survival by keeping their costs and business risks down. They want a win-win too. Presenting a less-onerous service agreement to a client prospect can be part of a strong win-win marketing strategy. If a client has the freedom to exit a one-year agreement early, without penalty—if for example your service levels are not what was promised— that may be the "win" that allows a prospect to sign an agreement with you and not one of your competitors.

When a few clients inevitably broke our service agreement, I was able to negotiate a settlement or make good on any shortfalls in our service in 95% of the disputes. Developing my win-win negotiating skills with clients and learning how to best deliver on our service promises was far more valuable than an "air-tight" paper contract. When I couldn't negotiate a win-win dispute resolution, I just let them go.

I'm not recommending that you operate without a signed service agreement. I'm recommending you use one that's short, easily readable, defines your services and your client's payment terms. The services contract you use is a key building block in your client relationship and a prime win-win negotiating opportunity at the start of a relationship. Your service contracts also affect your company's future valuation. Operating without a signed contract shows you are fearful, not confident of your services, and you permanently cede the upper hand to your client in future negotiations.

When I sold my business, all my clients and their service contracts transitioned successfully to the new owner.

Even in a larger company, you should work to get your legal team to reduce the size of a "standard contract" if you engage with them in a win-win atmosphere and explain what your team is trying to achieve. I was able to do this by bringing an "agreement draft" to my meetings with our legal team. They did end up adding a few paragraphs, but their changes were trivial compared to the "standard corporate agreement" that our legal team would have started with if I didn't bring my own draft.

Win-win negotiating when hiring

You have one "first time" to negotiate with a job prospect and set the tone for your relationship with that person if they become a new employee—a tone which will likely last for the duration of her employment on your team. If you show that you're willing to offer a win-win opportunity to your new employees, from your very first meeting, then you've set the appropriate tone for the remainder of a potentially fruitful relationship. Paying top dollar for talent is not a smart strategy, but negotiating for top talent is. If you overpay for your employees, or as a business owner you effectively trade your own fair compensation in an attempt to entice a key employee to come on board or stay on your team— you've set the stage for an inevitable day of reckoning. You don't want to feel resentful that someone else is receiving the compensation of a team leader or a business owner, with few of the burdens. Down the road, they'll resent and sabotage your inevitable future need to bring their compensation back in line with the market rate for their talent.

Here are two ways that I negotiate for win-win when hiring key staff members:

1. Hire someone who might one-day buy you out or replace you as the team leader.

As a small business owner, this strategy gives you leverage in establishing an affordable compensation package, and gives the new hire a powerful reason to stay with your company during the tumultuous first few years. It gives your key new team member something to dream about, talk to their spouse about, and remain motivated and persistent during times of stress. It's a fair win-win negotiating strategy for the new employee as well, to accept a lower-than-market-rate compensation in exchange for the opportunity of potentially owning the company in five to ten years.

As a team leader of a corporate department, you should do the equivalent in the sense of ensuring that you have groomed someone to take over if you get promoted. This may seem risky to your career, but it shows your confidence in your ability and elicits the highest performance from a key team member as she learns to trust that you have her best interest in mind as well as your own.

2. Recognize the non-cash negotiating items that you can use in lieu of a higher compensation.

The promise of an early job performance review, flexible work hours or start times, the opportunity to work from a home office for a few days, specialized industry training offered by your company, rotating job responsibilities, and even the positive vibes that existing team members can impart to the new employee—these are all good negotiating points to help you contain the compensation burden for your team when you are hiring. Staying at or under a "salary cap" is a good way to leave room in your budget to hire another staff member—without requesting an increase in your departmental budget or requiring you to accept less in compensation if you're the owner.

In fact, I recommend that you only bring people onto your team who are responsive to a win-win bargain, and seem appreciative of the opportunity. If you overpay someone right from the start, you can't subsequently reduce their pay without serious consequences for your company. You'll probably have to eventually fire anyone who was initially overpaid based on the market rate for their skill and then subsequently had their pay reduced. If this happens, it opens the door for potential sabotage.

Your overall awareness and positive attitude is the key to win-win negotiating success

Many people don't like conflict, so they avoid it whenever possible. I've seen it over and over in every position I've held. I believe everyone has to come to terms with negotiating; it's an invaluable skill. Personally, I never shied away from negotiating, but I used to be unconcerned about what the other party received, as long as I got what I wanted. When I was a newly hired college graduate, I negotiated a starting salary slightly higher than a female colleague, hired at the same time, who simply accepted what was offered. When she eventually learned that I and other new hires had negotiated our starting salaries, she of course felt buyers' remorse and grew frustrated. She hadn't realized the negotiating opportunity she had entered.

In order to put win-win negotiation into practice, you first have to recognize how you can arrange to be in a win-win negotiating situation. Increasing your awareness of the potential for a deal is the foundational first step of attaining win-win skill mastery. Remember our BOLD Success Principle: "Success follows a predictable course. It's not the brightest who succeed, or those presented with a perfect opportunity. Success follows those who have been given ordinary opportunities—and who have the presence of mind and the courage to seize them." As an entrepreneur, corporate executive, or intrapreneurial team leader, if you aren't aware of negotiating opportunities and don't begin to master win-win strategies, you will likely not succeed in achieving your objectives.

Again, I'm not saying that you should give in to what others want from you; that's not win-win. It has to work both ways, so you also get something better. Even in your own daily life, just accepting what's offered is easy, as there's little conflict. But if you accept only what's offered, and don't try to negotiate an even better deal, you'll be paying far too much for some major purchases in your life—like your car and your house, and even leaving potential income on the table when negotiating compensation for a job. Without win-win negotiating, you're underselling your own and your team's talents in the marketplace, and likely not maximizing your success opportunities. But the same is true in reverse, if you don't give other people what they need in the negotiation, they won't cooperate with you, and chances are, you need their cooperation in order to succeed.

The best negotiations result in *everyone* winning something valuable and no lingering sense of "buyer's remorse." That is how win-win negotiation differs from traditional notions of negotiation, where one person wins and the other loses. When someone loses, they never forget it; they become increasingly resentful, and may attempt to sabotage the agreement at some inopportune time in the future.

Business leaders who are not expert win-win negotiators, or are not committed to becoming an expert, are putting their company's or team's success at serious risk. Win-win negotiation is how better-than-average odds at achieving success happen. Those who have a sensitive awareness of negotiating opportunities in all areas of their business and their personal lives will propel themselves down the path of repeatable success. The only way to gain this awareness is to practice getting what you need, while allowing others to get what they need as well.

What if the other party won't negotiate for a win-win?

There is usually something that can be negotiated to achieve a win-win, but sometimes the other party feels they have no need to negotiate with you. They may see themselves in a stronger position and believe that "you have no choice but to work with them." Or you may represent an insignificant revenue base to them and they don't mind if they lose your business. Either way, by noticing their negotiating tactics, you can learn something about the other party. If you suspect they are unwilling to offer you a win-win deal, then the best strategy is to suspend the negotiation for a "few days." Don't say when you will get back to them; just leave the "cooling off" timeframe vague. Half the time, the other party will come back to you, once you've moved away from the negotiating table, and offer their own concession ideas. For example, you will see this happen quite often when negotiating with a car dealer.

If the other party doesn't come back to the table first, then bring the situation to an outside advisor or subject it to a brainstorming session with your team before you re-engage with the other party. Try to find something new to go back to the negotiating table with. It's usually not just about negotiating money, as other items or terms of value will often get the deal done. Give it one more creative try, and then be prepared to move on.

However, there are times that even when you're consciously pursuing a win-win negotiation, the other party may sabotage it, demanding a win-lose scenario. Sometimes there's nothing you can do to show them a better way. But as far as it's up to you, make sure there's a way that all partners to a negotiation can cede some points, and still win.

If you must, walk away from a deal that doesn't leave you with a win-win flavor. Your instincts about the other party are usually well-founded and often turn out to be self-fulfilling. This happened to me when I was negotiating to purchase a business similar to my own, with the intent of growing and expanding it through acquisition. At a late hour of the negotiation, the other party changed the deal, so I had to suspend the negotiation. He became upset with this change of events and began negotiating with another buyer, which was fine with me. I didn't want to feel that I was negotiating with someone who wanted a win for himself and a loss for me.

Some people will never be satisfied unless they not only win it all, but you lose. When you realize you're negotiating with someone who holds this trait, then your only options are either to withdraw from the negotiation, suspend it temporarily in a "cool down" period, or to capitulate. We hope you don't choose the last option. It's always best to walk away entirely, with no buyer's remorse, no future day-of-reckoning, and negotiate a better deal with another party, on another day.

Above all, don't let fear negotiate for you. If you become fearful during a negotiation, remember what your team's BOLD purpose is, what your personal BOLD purpose is—and stay true to them. Without having many prior years of win-win negotiating practice, it would have been easy to let fear do the negotiating for me, on one Sunday night when my company's future was on the line and I had to make a decision to sell my business or not. (You'll read about that night in the final chapter discussing BOLDskill 10). I didn't allow fear to take a seat at the negotiating table that night. Instead, I used my win-win negotiating skills to regain my perspective and my optimism—there just had to be a way we could both win.

With enough practice, you'll be able to recognize win-win negotiating opportunities, assess the key needs of your counterpart, your team, as well as your own needs—and boldly act to negotiate deals that allow you and your team to accomplish seemingly impossible goals. You can use the Win-Win Negotiating Worksheet in Appendix M.

BOLD takeaways

- Win-win negotiating awareness is similar to opportunity awareness. The team leader needs to become aware of situations that offer win-win negotiating opportunities.

- There is usually something that the other party to the negotiation wants or needs in order to achieve a win-win agreement. It's your job to put yourself in their shoes and figure out what it is and how you can give it to them.

- Even if you think you negotiated a win for yourself, if the other person feels they lost, they'll sabotage the deal later. Everyone hates losing and everyone has experienced buyers' remorse, so always negotiate for a win-win.

- Many interactions with your peers and in your daily life are opportunities for win-win negotiation, if you've practiced enough and developed your negotiation awareness.

- Win-win negotiation is a strategic tool that can remove an obstacle and open an innovative pathway to success. Leaders of Surging Teams use win-win negotiation in all aspects of their business and personal lives.

- Having win-win relationships enlarges your sphere of influence and broadens your "base of friendly minds" whom you can enlist to contribute innovative ideas when your team encounters a success obstacle—and you need a creative solution to win.

- Never agree to a win-lose deal. It's better to suspend the negotiation or walk away entirely, than to accept a win-lose deal.

Make peace with fear and doubt

I learned that courage was not the absence of fear, but the triumph over it. The brave man is not he who does not feel afraid, but he who conquers that fear.
—NELSON MANDELA

The following conversation happened between our Public Relations (PR) vendor and me, shortly after I won the "Franchise of the Year" award from the franchise company headquarters.

"I really hate the alarm clock each morning," admitted Jack, our assigned PR account exec.

"I haven't used an alarm clock since I opened my business," I replied.

Jack was curious, "Why not?"

"Because each morning, when I open my eyes, I'm gripped by the fear of what I need to accomplish today—and I practically leap out of bed regardless of the time!" I explained.

Jack considered that for a moment and looked intently at me. "I want to feel that sense of urgency and passion for my own work," he confided.

My anecdote of "leaping out of bed" was meant to describe the power of my business owner fears to Jack. But it had a different effect on him. To Jack, it sounded desperately attractive, especially to someone who was secretly longing for meaning and challenge in their own work-life. Not long after the conversation, Jack opened his own PR business, and never looked back.

Learn to embrace fear, but unrelenting fear is debilitating

Having a healthy dose of fear is motivational, so embrace it. For some people, like Jack the PR Guy above, the stress of owning a business can feel like a stimulant, especially in the early days. It results in a mild dose of fear that jolts them to come alive with renewed energy. But for many entrepreneurs, the unrelenting stress related to owning a business can result in constant fears that eventually become debilitating if they're not recognized and countered. These unrelenting fears eventually caught up to me when I owned my franchise business.

Scene: My doctor's office
The door opened, and the doctor walked back in.

"You've been here once before, Scott. Do you remember?" he said.

I was surprised and sure it wasn't true, "No, I don't remember," I said.

"It was in 1988, do you remember now?" he said.

Given that was decades ago, I searched my memory and finally placed the event. "Oh, It was when I was getting divorced," I said.

The doctor looked at me and waited for me to understand what this really meant as far as my malady was concerned.

"So, you're saying this is a stress-induced problem then?" I deduced.

"Yes, it appears so," he confirmed.

I remembered recently having to pull over while driving to a client's office. I had to close my eyes and try to clear my vision, which seemed to be scrolling like an old analog TV screen that wasn't tuned in correctly. I'd also recently experienced recurring throat tightening, and that was what finally compelled me to make time in my schedule to attend this doctor's appointment.

Years earlier, while working for a division of GE and charged with the intrapreneurial role of leading a team to develop the discount dining program I've discussed in this book, I began to experience intermittent chest tightening. It became so intense that when I finally visited a local physician, he panicked and told me to go immediately to the emergency room of a local hospital. After numerous stress tests, and a visit from my concerned, young wife, the results came back negative for any heart condition. The culprit was identified as job-related stress.

Thankfully none of my stress-related maladies thus far have been a precursor of a heart attack or other serious physical condition. But all of them were definitely physiological reactions to unrelenting stress. They were almost as debilitating as an actual disease, and even a doctor couldn't readily tell them apart. Do you think a business leader who's experiencing this kind of stress will be "on top of his game?"

Rely on your formal business plan if you are breaching your financial comfort zone

If you are an entrepreneur, your biggest stressor is likely going to be over your financial investment, and your biggest fear is the loss of that investment. Money has a way to make people feel sick. Sure, everyone will line up to congratulate you when you're rolling in profits, but losses are isolating. It's hard to find enthusiastic support from peers when your company seems to be bleeding cash.

TIPS TO CONSCIOUSLY "LET GO"
WHEN FEAR BECOMES PRESSURE

Balance your life with activities designed to relieve stress and address your constant fears. This is the "P" in PERMA, Positive emotions in your life. Be alert for the stress reactions your body and mind produce when you're under constant, self-induced pressure. Your body and mind can begin to treat your self-induced pressure like it treats fear, and gears you up for either "fight" or "flight."

When you notice these symptoms of stress, it's time to disengage for a while and rest, or at least add positive and enjoyable activities to your daily and weekly routines. Leaders are tough, but they're usually toughest on themselves. Don't be the worst boss you ever had. Take a few days off; go away on a 3-day weekend. Take a full-week vacation. Whatever you do, give yourself some regular time away—you deserve it and so does your family.

My response to the "throat tightening" event was to plan a vacation that forced me to disengage from my business and rest my mind and emotions. By the time I returned, my symptoms were gone. So think about what you can do to break your debilitating cycle of stress, and free yourself from constant fears. If you can't just disengage and take a vacation, find some other outlet to relax.

In those times, your best source of hope is to know that your business plan was drafted with astute objectivity, and that you will eventually succeed if the plan is followed. (This is also a good reason to ensure that you have written a formal, well-thought out business plan.) When you're running an aggressive, costly marketing campaign, or are in a growth posture that requires you to spend money, your plan will have already factored in the upfront costs of these revenue-generating efforts. Knowing that you already planned for these pressures should help relieve some stress and take pressure off you—if you trust your plan. Following a thoughtfully prepared "best case, worst case, & likely case" business plan, which clearly outlines a pro-forma financial statement and timeline for when the business will breakeven, and thus no longer require your further personal investment—can be a great help.

Sometimes, even with a formal business plan, the entrepreneur's personal "financial comfort zone" can feel breached, and your plan now seems like a fanciful musing. That's when the fear "of losing everything" begins to make recurring, debilitating appearances. If this happens, the healthiest perspective an entrepreneur can take is to view this as investing in yourself through growing your business and generating a return that will far outweigh the initial investment.

If you focus solely on the outflow of your capital and credit, and "give up" on the expectation of healthy financial returns, you will jump off the success track and end up on the road toward business failure. Your recurring thoughts of "losing it all" will actually begin to dictate self-fulfilling actions of failure. This is one reason why spending time thinking through, writing down, and developing a formal business plan is so important, and why it's one of our BOLDskills. Filling your mind with a well-thought out business plan can help to counteract those dark thoughts of failure.

Entrepreneurs must remember that it isn't a zero-sum game: spending money to grow the company vs. having less savings for your future. Instead, consider any spending from your personal savings toward your business as an investment that will result in net profits and a greater return on your investment than your savings account or other financial vehicles could have ever generated.

If you start a business and draw an investment line, vowing never to touch those funds and credit beyond that line for business use, you will likely face a crisis. Rarely does a business owner stay within the money initially set aside as the required start-up capital. If the thought of this makes you feel ill, then don't move forward with starting a business, and save yourself an anxiety attack, or even a divorce.

I hope this advice may save some people their marriage. If your spouse is not in favor of your new business endeavor, then you need to seriously consider the potential consequences of moving forward. I've seen marriages unravel during the business start-up phase, and the risks of a divorce caused by your new business (or a business failure caused by a divorce) are a real and present relational danger.

For Intrapreneurs: Managing the fear of losing your corporate job

Many of the same fears, risks and stresses of the entrepreneur are present if you're leading a corporate business unit. You'll be competing with the sometimes ferocious leaders of other business units and perhaps with corporate senior executives for scarce company resources. Many times your requests for finite company resources will be in direct competition with them. Senior executives will be ruthless in getting those resources for their units, and they will come directly after you with the intent of getting you to drop your requests or to get you to agree to give their unit priority. Fear of losing your corporate job will be just as real to you as the "fear of financial ruin" is to the entrepreneur. I have learned that corporate politics can trump personal relationships, especially when you consider the kind of personality and political capabilities it takes to reach the senior power ranks of a large organization. Here's a real story of a power struggle that happened to me.

"Peter isn't a big fan of the dining program," said my corporate attorney friend, as we jogged together.

"What do you mean?" I said.

"We just had an executive committee meeting, and Peter was adamant that the company was wasting its financial investment on the dining program. He called it a boondoggle. Peter recommended to the committee that *his* new program be given some of the investment that's currently committed to develop the dining program," continued my friend.

Peter was and is still a personal friend of mine, but corporate friendships are complex and sometimes combative. There is a hierarchy that a corporation needs in order to execute its evolutionary change strategies in the marketplace, and corporate friendships exist within this hierarchy. Although Peter had helped me in my career, and provided me with opportunities for promotion and influence, he had his own corporate team and objectives. The pursuit of our respective team's objectives had for now positioned us as rivals for the limited budget allowed for funding new products. I understood the implications of this relational complexity by how it played out in the boardroom. In the end, the Dining Program received the funding it needed to continue its growth, and Peter and I have remained friends.

If you haven't yet experienced internal corporate threats and opposition, either implied or direct, from angry senior company executives, or even from friendly colleagues—then you either aren't seriously trying to succeed in achieving success, or you will soon experience these threats as you implement the BOLDskills ideas in this book. When your division begins to succeed, and it requires more company resources to drive your team all the way over the finish line, you'll feel pressures you never even imagined existed. Your career may be in jeopardy, and you may not even realize it. You can't eliminate these threats when you are trying to lead a team to win in highly competitive situations. The stakes are financial success, professional notoriety, executive power—and scarce company resources.

Learn to calm your mind, allay fears, stay healthy, and "stay in your 3-foot world"

Learning to live with and overcome fears is something each person has to accomplish in their own life. Maslow's famous Hierarchy of Needs pyramid (on page 15 in chapter "What is a Surging Team") shows us that in order to reach higher levels of emotional health, self-esteem, and self-actualization—we must first learn to deal with our fears. Of course, team leaders and company owners must learn to cope with more intense fears than non-team-leaders; it comes with their job. Effective leaders must learn new methods to cope with the escalated fears that come with ever more responsibility. If they don't, then their teams will will fail to achieve their potential.

To prepare yourself to coexist, I recommend that you maintain an exercise program, and jealously guard the time you need each day to remain physically and mentally fit. So many times the answer to a vexing negotiating conundrum became clear when I shifted my mind away from the immediate problem and focused on physical exertion.

Yoga and meditation are also very helpful to divert the focus of your attention away from the problems vexing you. Chicago Bulls and LA Lakers coach, Phil Jackson, was nicknamed "the Zen Master" for the way he used meditation as a tool to help both him and his teams cope with the stress of leading them to almost a dozen world championships (if you combine the two teams he coached). Christians in business can meditate on 2 Timothy 1:7 as a verse to deal with fear:

> *"You have not been given a spirit of fear,*
> *but a spirit of power, love, and a sound mind."*

As a practical fear-fighting technique, I suggest you take the advice of Mark Owen, retired Navy Seal, and a man who knows about fear. As he wrote in his book, *No Easy Day*, when he described the fears that one encounters in rock climbing, "Look, you can't affect anything outside of three feet around you, can you? So stay in your three-foot world. Look inside your three-foot world, find the next hand hold, and climb your way out."

Playing off Owen's "rock climbing analogy," I offer the following 7-step plan for entrepreneurial and intrapreneurial leaders to face and embrace their fears:

1. Start with optimism & excitement, just as a climber does.

2. Once you face your obstacles (your personal cliff-overhang), let your excitement become focused determination.

3. When obstacles are more formidable than expected, be prepared for determination to turn into fear and regret: "Why did I ever start to climb this rock!"

4. If you don't address this fear and regret—you will freeze, grow weak, and eventually fall.

5. Adjust your thinking to "stay in your three-foot world." Just move one handhold forward each day on the way to climbing past immediate obstacles.

6. Regroup and rededicate yourself to achieving your original objective of "climbing over the cliff."

7. Once the business success objective is achieved, and you've "climbed over the cliff," the leader enjoys a new wisdom, and can embrace forgiveness—forgiveness for anyone whom you feel should have helped you more as you climbed, anyone who tried to make you fall, and even for yourself for not initially anticipating or possessing the needed "rock climbing" skills.

On days when you experience debilitating fears, stay in your three-foot world and do something within your reach that day. Learn our BOLDskills for Accelerated Team Success and put your learnings into practice each day to move one handhold closer to your goal. Don't worry about tomorrow; you can only affect what's happening in the "now." Your business plan has already contemplated for "tomorrow," so just follow it today.

To begin working with your stress and fears, use this Fear Response Worksheet to help you stay in your three-foot world and take your next handhold forward. You might want to write your answers to the Fear Response Worksheet in your own private diary or journal.

FEAR RESPONSE WORKSHEET

1.	What is the fear that is interfering with your team's objectives?
2.	Can you adjust your thinking to "stay in your three-foot world" and just move one handhold forward today, on the way to climbing past your immediate fear obstacle?
3.	Does your business plan or your 100–day Action Plan show you the way past the fear?
4.	Can you maintain your original company objectives, even in the face of this fear?
5.	Can you engage your team in brainstorming to source some innovative ideas to move past the current fear while staying on track for achieving your team goals? If not with your team, can your friends or advisors provide some ideas
6.	Think about breathing in and out and how good it feels to fill your lungs with fresh air, and then to slowly exhale. You can also use physical exercise to gain this extended period of mental rest, by pursuing an exercise routine that forces you to concentrate on the exercise, on your next breath, and recovering from your physical fatigue. When you return from this mental rest, you will be better able to face your fear. What type of exercise are you willing and able to do?
7.	Plan some time to get away from work and rest your mind. Don't use this time to think about the solution to your current fear, just rest your mind. If you can't get away, spend some time meditating or praying, but rest your mind from thinking about this current fear and just focus on meditation or three current blessings in your life for an extended period of time. Write down where you might enjoy getting away and how you can set up the time to do it. If not a trip, write down your commitment to begin meditating.
8.	Also use the ABCDE Exercise for Identifying and Overcoming Fear provided in Appendix F.

BOLD takeaways

- A leader will inevitably face some fears. A healthy dose of fear can be stimulating and not necessarily debilitating, so learn to embrace some fears as healthy.

- Jealously guard time to regularly rest your mind and body, so you can sustain a determined and passionate success drive—until your team wins.

- Follow the path you thoughtfully created with your business plan. Preparing a well-thought out annual business plan, and using it to guide your business decisions, is critical to helping you feel less fear, especially when your comfort zone is breached.

- Reframe your thinking about losing your investment into the positive attitude that you are investing in yourself, and your investment will generate larger returns than if you had simply put your money into a savings account.

- When you are feeling like your fears are debilitating, learn to "stay in your three-foot world." Don't consider the larger strategic issues during these debilitating times. Just look for a safe place for your next step or to take your next handhold, and make one small move forward each day according to your plan.

- If you start to panic, consider what the worst case scenario is if your fears played out as you imagine they will. What is the absolute worst thing that can happen? How likely is this worst case to actually happen? Learn to argue effectively with yourself with facts to avoid panic. Use the ABCDE Exercise for Identifying and Overcoming Fear in Appendix F.

Become a BOLD salesperson for your business and your team

For every sale you miss because you were too enthusiastic, you'll miss a hundred because you weren't enthusiastic enough.

— ZIG ZIGLAR

Can you build a Surging Team, one that achieves unstoppable success, without some sales being made somewhere along the way?

Of course not! It's absurd to think so.

This isn't a book on sales; it's a book on developing an unstoppable Surging Team. But selling is an important skill on your team, and is similar to win-win negotiating. Once you change your mindset about selling and negotiating, they both can become fun and anticipated games—not tasks to be fearful about. Even if you don't know your prospect's exact business needs, you do know that you're a smart and savvy executive, business owner, or professional consultant. You are an asset to any company who hires you—and you come with a great team to back you up.

Beware of negative self-talk. You can't outsell your mindset, so if you tell yourself you can't sell, or you're afraid of asking for a sale, then you won't be very effective. Try using one of your top five signature character strengths to help prepare yourself before you go into a sales situation, by considering how you can use that strength during your coming sales conversation. People will respond positively when you act like you're sincerely enjoying the conversation.

As a small business owner, you are your #1 salesperson

Too many small business owners are told or believe that they can outsource the critical sales role in their company. The sooner you debunk that myth, accept the ultimate sales responsibility for your company, and get started learning how to be a BOLD salesman for your team—the sooner your business will achieve success.

I've watched dozens of my peer business owners repeatedly attempt to train a successful salesperson, and I know that very few succeeded. I can count them on one hand, with a few fingers still tucked away. Sometimes the salesperson hangs on because the owner really wants them to succeed, but in the end, the salesperson doesn't generate enough sales sufficient to cover his salary, and the owner must divert his own critical time and energy to the "firing process" which is messy, emotionally taxing, and risky to your business. Yes, firing a salesperson is risky. If the owner is spending considerable time trying to train and otherwise "save" their underperforming salesperson, then this is time the owner is not spending on actual sales and company growth.

But there is more risk to hiring salespeople than just the opportunity cost to the business of the owner diverting his precious time hiring and firing. People don't like to be fired, so they often get angry and sometimes they use all their energy to hurt your business to "get even." If you stay away from trying to hire a salesperson prematurely from day one, you won't have to fire them on day 90, or if you're really stubborn, on day 120. I have no doubt that's about how long they'll last, unless you're even more stubborn than me.

WHAT IF YOU AND YOUR TEAM DON'T DIRECTLY COME INTO CONTACT WITH CUSTOMERS OR EVEN PROSPECTS?

If your team is operational in nature, you may think you're not involved in sales, so this BOLDskill does not pertain to you as a leader. However, it's likely that you can make a contribution to sales. For example, many times the technical and operational staff of your prospects are invited to a sales meeting, and they have been given "veto power." They're encouraged to come prepared with "gotcha" questions and "rattle" the appointed salesperson. Their input sometimes forces sales concessions, or it can even thwart the deal if the salesperson isn't prepared to respond confidently. When I was a corporate team leader of technical and operational staff, I was asked to join our sales executives for just that reason—to help defend them against these "operations plants."

"Scott, I know that the prospect's technical and operations team leaders will be attending our sales meeting, so would it be possible for you join our sales team to answer their questions?" Over time, I gained a reputation as "user-friendly software engineer," and this trait was recognized as potentially valuable by the sales team for my division. It turned out to be my key to unlocking an entire new world, one where I participated in client sales meetings. I also got to work with the most powerful executives in my company.

But if you really believe that your team is isolated from the actual sale, then your team isn't very valuable to the company, and your team will likely be one of the first required to downsize during the next budget cycle. So my advice is to get your team involved with sales fast—as teams that are seen as key to the sales efforts are usually the last ones involved in a downsizing.

I know this from experience, and the following story shows what's likely to happen.

Sylvia's eyes teared up immediately as I sat down. I think she knew that it just wasn't working out, but I wasn't positive that she knew. So we were meeting this morning at the coffee shop, just like we had met each of the prior 3 weeks, reviewing performance from the prior week—but today I was going to fire her. I chose a public place to fire Sylvia, so that there would be witnesses if there were any problems. This is especially true if I intend to fire someone.

"I'm sorry . . . ," she said.

"I'm sorry, too, but it didn't work out," I said quietly but firmly. "You can just leave your equipment and paperwork here with me. You'll be getting two weeks of severance pay as long as you sign this agreement that you won't contact any of our clients or prospects." I put the agreement in front of her, and she signed it without even reading it.

"Is there anything else?" she asked?

"No, that's all."

Sylvia slowly collected herself, got up, and walked out of the café. I watched her go. She was the last of the salespeople that I had hired in the early days of running my new franchise business. They each started out so optimistically and saw this as a new adventure. But it didn't take long, maybe a couple of months, before they started to grow weary with rejection. Our conversations were never as upbeat as that first month, and inevitably there comes the day when the cost of their salary—even a small salary—became unjustifiable.

On this day, I sat for a while after Sylvia left, before taking a deep breath and heading back to my home office. Sylvia would be our last salesperson. After she left, I took on the Chief Sales Officer position myself, and never looked back. I now know that If I didn't step into that role and succeed, then my company would have failed.

The lesson you have to learn here is that hiring a salesperson, before you achieve significant sales and profitability for your small business, will increase your risk of business failure. You need to focus your time and talent on learning how to be a BOLD salesman for your business, and lead your team to achieve profitable business performance as soon as possible. Do this before you ever consider hiring a salesperson.

The role of a salesperson in our franchise businesses was a topic regularly debated among my business owner peer-collaboration group. For me and almost all my colleagues, the end result of hiring a salesperson prematurely was always the failure of the salesperson and a revenue shortfall. Why? Because who do you think is more motivated to overcome repeated rejections and make a sale for your company: you or a hired salesperson?

For those of us who were trained in other disciplines, sales is a skill we have to acquire on-the-job. But once we accept that we can indeed learn to sell, our subject matter business expertise actually helps us relate better to our prospects, who are usually weary of being approached by professional salespeople.

This book is focused on what you can do to achieve *reliably repeatable* team and company success. You are in the best position to become a BOLD and effective salesperson for your team. I've seen it happen many times—when the owner seizes the top sales role, the company jolts forward toward success with renewed energy. Conversely, when an owner abdicates or delegates the sales role, the company stalls.

So let's be honest here. If you really feel that you are not capable of sales, answer these questions. Are you prepared to hire a proven, effective salesperson? Are you prepared to hire a salesperson that you believe has the potential to earn as much or more than you do as the company owner? If yes, you'll have to pay handsomely for it. The best salespeople are highly compensated, and this is what helps to keep them moving past sales barriers, rejections, and on to continue making the next sales call. Or are you planning to hire someone you believe you can afford, and hope they can generate sales and cover their own costs?

The latter scenario was recommended to me by my former franchisor, and so I hired a string of six inexperienced and low-cost salespeople who made one or two sales and then became ineffective, each and every one. They were not experienced enough to know how to maintain a consistently effective sales performance, and if they were, I wouldn't have hired them because they would have required a higher compensation than I could afford. They'd barely made enough sales to cover their own costs. Meanwhile, I was not gaining my own sales experience, and I was left with a chaotic sales effort. Even worse, my company was now ominously behind schedule in achieving our breakeven point. This is exactly how companies fail, especially start-ups.

So that is the conundrum. You can hire the top salespeople and pay them more than you are earning and never make a profit. Or you can hire lower-cost salespeople and you will never get anywhere. Neither one is a good choice.

Some people think they can hire a friend or even a close relative to join their company and fill the critical sales role—and that this will address the sales conundrum I discussed above. But many times, I've seen my peers lose control of their business through the betrayal of a close relative or even a former "best" friend. These trusted people were empowered by the owner to "make the sale" and maintain the customer relationships, while the owner "ran the company." Whoever makes the sale is in the most influential position with your clients, and sometimes trusted people use this influence to steal your clients and ruin your company.

Don't set yourself up to lose control of your business out of "blind trust" for a friend or relative. Money and power are notorious corrupters, and you may end up losing a friend, damaging an important family relationship, and losing your company as well. This scenario of betrayal was one of the most common reasons that several of my franchise business owner colleagues quickly went out of business.

There is no other role in your company that impacts your success as directly as sales. Ask yourself why would you delegate this role during your company's most critical period? Whatever the answer, do what you must to overcome your fear of sales, so you can begin your journey to become a BOLD salesperson for your company. You want to be certain that you did everything you possibly could to personally achieve your company's success objectives. Learning to become a BOLD salesperson is a skill that you as the entrepreneur must embrace and master to drive your Surging Team past your company's success goals. You can't afford not to.

I hate selling, what should I do?

Some owners simply don't like to go on initial sales calls, and feel that their time is better spent operating the business. Others will only go if it's a large opportunity. I've heard all the rationalizations for these excuses, but none are very good.

You can and should use many lead generation channels, including hiring someone to make initial phone calls or to send marketing materials to surface leads. But you need to embrace that fact that one of your key roles as the owner is your role as the Chief Sales Officer and embrace every opportunity to walk into a prospect's business and show them how your company can help them succeed. Going on sales calls keeps you in front of prospects and assures that you understand how they respond to your marketing campaigns. It also assures that you get to know any objections made to your sales efforts, and it alerts you to potential upsell opportunities that you may not have thought about before. Who is the most motivated person in your company to look for a second and a third sale to a new client? You!

As I pointed out in the negotiation chapter, Malcolm Gladwell explained in his book, *Outliers,* that in order to become an expert at something, you need to practice for about 10,000 hours. That's about five years of full time work at 2,000 hours per year. So I encourage you, the small business owner or team leader not to delay. Embrace the challenge and start today to achieve your own BOLD sales expertise.

UNDOING YOUR FEAR OF SALES

If you've convinced yourself that you hate the sales role, here are some ideas you can try to reverse this mindset:

1. Use the 100–day Sales Action Plan Template in Appendix G to develop the steps you need to achieve significant revenues within that period.

2. Begin by pretending you just hired yourself for a 100% commission sales job, and you have to get very good at it as fast as you can to start generating revenue, or your company will fail.

3. Resolve to spend the next 100 days developing your sales skills, while following a plan designed to significantly increase your company's revenues. Resolve to stay in this "three-foot sales world" for the entire 100 days.

4. Now, determine how many sales you want to make in 100 days, multiply by 5, and use this as the number of face-to-face prospect visits you need to make in order to achieve your sales goals.

5. For 100 days, avoid any other use of your time other than marketing and selling to the number of prospects you calculated.

There are so many time wasters you build into your day, just because you like to do them. Be vigilant when non-sales distractions surface and set them aside. Learn to quickly mourn their loss (if it's one of your favorite time-wasting activities) or at least ignore them for the next 100 days until you've finished a complete 100–day sales plan!

6. Dress nicely! Plenty of studies show that dressing nicely is a major sales success factor. It's also a component of personal happiness, which is the "P" in PERMA. So, look in the mirror and tell yourself that you look like the greatest salesperson in the world. Then go look a prospect in the eyes and ask for a sale.

7. Get ready to laugh at your mistakes and ineptness. Don't take yourself too seriously. You'll improve and nobody has to die in order for you to gain valuable sales experience!

8. Enjoy the process. As you will discover, most prospects enjoy talking to other business owners who are not professional salespeople.

In the end, if you as the business owner can't BOLDLY and effectively sell your products and services, then your company will most likely fail to achieve success. That should be your ultimate motivation.

Tips on using cold calling to begin your BOLD salesperson transformation

When you cold call prospects, you find out fast that busy people cringe when you walk into their business, as soon as they realize what the objective of your visit is. You literally have about 7 seconds to make a great impression before you're sent on your way.

During my franchise business training, our sales coach, Veronica, had us practice our "elevator speech" and our business introduction. We practiced on each other in class, and it was quite fun—until we were actually on our way to cold call on some live prospects. I started to get nervous, but tried to keep a BOLD front. Here's how I decided to use my 7 seconds:

> *"Hi, I'm Scott Brennan and I'm the owner of a new computer service company in the area, CMIT Solutions. I'd like to talk to the owner about how we can help his company succeed."*

Sounds easy, right? But look in the mirror and without a script, try to say that a few times and insert your name and the name of your company. Even if you get this introduction mastered, you'll find that the response from the person in front of you is usually pretty discouraging. You won't feel very impressed with yourself after a few hours of cold calling. It's humbling and could be fatally discouraging, unless you consider it just 7 seconds in your quest to gain 10,000 hours of sales practice. That's a lot of sales calls and elevator speeches.

Overcoming the imposter syndrome

When I started to cold call as part of my sales effort for my business, I felt inauthentic, as if I was role playing and pretending to be someone that I wasn't. This feeling caught me off-guard. Here I was an accomplished business professional, and yet I felt like I was faking my identity. Eventually, as I gained practice and gained a few clients, I was able to overcome that feeling.

If you feel this way, too, I suggest you Google the term "imposter syndrome," and you'll find many articles about it. One article from Forbes, "Afraid of Being 'Found Out'? How to Overcome Imposter Syndrome" offers some good insights to counteract the imposter syndrome, which I will summarize here:

- Think closely about why you feel inauthentic. If you are honest with yourself, you'll come to realize that the only impostor you ever had to worry about is your fear of people thinking you are one.

- High achievers tend to focus on what they haven't accomplished, versus feeling proud of what they have done. So if you are a high achiever, driving yourself to ever-greater heights, you have to take a moment to remember the great things you have already done. Once you do that, you will know you are not an imposter.

Even if you're convinced that cold calling prospects is a poor marketing channel, I highly recommend that you spend some time meeting your prospects face-to-face, in impromptu situations, introducing yourself, your company, and deftly answering their objections. Train your mind to like the sound of your own voice, as you declare yourself and your company a trusted business resource your prospect can count on. This will help you learn to believe in yourself.

You can also assemble a "leave behind" package for your prospects containing some company "interest items" and a small gift for your prospects. Choose 25 prospects you'd love to turn into clients, stop by and leave your package, including your gift. It makes cold calling a little easier to do if you're stopping by to "drop off a gift." You should always ask to speak to your target prospect while you're there, but if it's still anxiety-provoking for you, at least leave your package.

At the same time that you're practicing your cold calling introduction, and getting used to hearing your own voice, there's another "advanced cold calling" technique you must begin to use. You need to be sure to tell your prospect exactly how your company can help him and how he can buy from you. Just giving your company name and declaring your new business role isn't enough—you need to help the prospect understand why and how to buy from you.

Some top selling business coaches do not recommend cold calling. They consider it an inefficient use of your time, and recommend that you select another more efficient sales channel from the many sales channels available to you. For me, however, cold calling proved to be extremely valuable in developing my "success persona" as a business owner—and training my mind to hear me declare it and ultimately to believe it. In effect, cold calling helped me get over my feeling of being inauthentic and made me a much stronger business owner.

As you practice and develop your skills, listen for clues to make the sale

If you persist in your sales efforts, you'll eventually get opportunities to meet face-to-face with top prospects. However, you may only get one chance in front of these people, as setting up a follow-up appointment is impossible if they don't like what you have to offer the first time. So be prepared to ask them all the necessary questions about their business and let your prospect do most of the talking. Once you get them talking about their business, it may be hard to bring the conversation to an end, so you'll be in a favorable position to tell your prospect what your company can do for them and how they can buy from you.

Even if the prospect doesn't buy from you right there as you sit across from them, you made the best use of your one grand shot with them—by learning about their business, telling why they should buy from you, and then explaining how they can buy from you. Sometimes you can get the sale just by asking for it. It's happened to me, and it makes a lasting impression on your self-image as a BOLD salesperson.

You should always feel confident that any prospect you meet would be better off after hiring your company—especially because you also have the advantage of an unstoppable Surging Team to back you up.

Be sure to look for opportunities during the sales process to practice your win-win negotiating skills. The prospect will almost always provide clues to tell you how to sell to him—if you're listening closely. Detecting these clues made each sales opportunity fun for me, trying to find that win-win balance with each prospect. There are many ways to provide the prospect with a "win" other than to immediately agree to lower your prices, so listen for any clues they're giving you. They may ask about payment terms, delivery methods, and what's included in the product or service combination—these are all negotiating tools you can use. To start the negotiation, set the price bar higher than you're comfortable with in your mind, and train yourself to listen for what's important to the prospect and not immediately revert to lowering your fee when the prospect raises an objection.

When prospects ask you to come down on your prices, it sounds so easy to say yes, and you want so badly to just get the deal done. In fact, you probably have already convinced yourself that you want this client because your company needs the revenue and your team needs a win. You need a foot in the door and a lower price seems like just the right foot to jam in there. Clients always want to pay less, but it's up to you to learn how to convince them that you're proposing a fair deal for both parties. If you sell your services for a loss, you won't be successful as a company, so what good will it do your clients if you don't have enough net profit on your sales and are forced to go out of business down the road? You may be able to offer lower prices, but don't automatically do so. Instead, listen for other negotiation clues provided by the prospect.

When you get to show somebody something wonderful, it isn't a sales call at all

In my view, every team in an organization is involved in sales, and has a responsibility to help make those sales.

Our dining program sales team used to keep coming up with excuses for why they couldn't meet their sales goals. Each deal our sales team made required my team to develop and implement procedures to "process" the sale. At one point, our sales team began blaming our procedures for impeding their sales efforts, which was ludicrous, since our role followed the sales process. So as the director of operations, I decided to ride along on a few sales calls with some salespeople, so I could better understand how they were selling our national dining program to restaurants.

I was surprised at what occurred. When I was present at a prospect, along with my company's assigned salesperson, I found that many times the salesperson would defer to me during the early part of the negotiation with restaurant owners to explain the benefits of our program. To my surprise, I often ended up making the sale—when I thought I was just going to be "riding along"—and I *enjoyed* it.

I started to think about how this turnabout happened, and then it became clear. I was extremely confident about how our program worked, and why it was beneficial for the restaurant prospect to join our program. All I had to do was open my mouth to explain the wonderful benefits, and everyone could hear my passion. Soon enough, voilà—I began gaining a reputation as a BOLD company salesperson. I found that if I didn't think of these client prospect meetings as "a sales call," and instead just considered them "a chance to explain the wonderful benefits of our dining rewards program." After all, who doesn't like dining out at great restaurants, and what restaurant doesn't want to attract new patrons?

That was our BOLD Purpose, to introduce frequent diners to great restaurants, and increase world happiness! Ok, I added the world happiness part just now, but seriously, who doesn't?

This experience proved to be invaluable for me to acquire a level of expertise in "sales" I never imagined. I soon became a BOLD salesperson for our division and my team. As I developed an awareness of my real sales skills, and what sales actually are about, I found that I could also use my newly discovered skills inside our company. I knew our product, I knew my team, and I was passionate about the success of each. This combination made me a very determined and persuasive negotiator. Later on, I also realized that we needed even more persuasive negotiators, so I sent some of my key operations team members to also "ride along" with our internal sales team. The same "sales awakening" happened to them. Our sales team loved the initiative, and my surging corporate team became even more unstoppable.

Overcoming the fear of "overselling" what you "can't deliver"

If you find yourself fearful about selling something you're unsure if your team can deliver, ask yourself, "Wouldn't every prospect be better off by hiring your team?" I bet your answer is, "Of course they would!"

Using BOLDskill 1, transform your fear of "overselling of capabilities" situation into a "team success opportunity," and let your team brainstorm together to find a way to deliver the overpromised product or service. My team was always somehow able to accommodate some "slight" mistakes I made in my sales promises. Remember, we weren't trying to sell brain surgery equipment or missiles—it was a dining program! People eat at great restaurants, they pay their bill, they got a reward, and if they liked the experience, they came back! What was the worst problem I could possibly encounter by overselling our program? Not much. Besides, our Sr. VP "Jane" had already taught me a lesson that it was "my job" as the director of operations to make sure we delivered on our sales promises. I learned that I could bring any "sales promise challenges" to my team to solve, they always rose to the challenge.

The same might be true for you. Ask yourself: What's the worst that can happen to you during a sales discussion, even if you slightly overpromise (as long as it's not weapons systems or medical technology?) Somebody says "NO," So, big deal! Laugh it off! They might also say "YES."

BOLD takeaways

- There can be no Surging Team without some sales being made somewhere along the way. You can't outsell your mindset, so if you as the team leader are uncomfortable with sales, you need to consciously practice acquiring sales skills. This chapter points you in the right direction, as the team leader, to become a BOLD salesman for your team.

- Team leaders of non-sales teams can often become valuable participants in the sales process. Work with your peers in the sales department and find ways that your team can support the sales effort. You want your team looked at as critical to the company's revenue generating capability. If you're not, then you're expendable.

- In the process of overcoming feelings of "being an imposter" while making a sales presentation, you'll come to realize that the only impostor you ever had to worry about is your fear of people thinking you are one. Have confidence in your knowledge of how your product or service works as a bridge to communicating with your prospects.

- Sales doesn't feel like sales when you think of it as an opportunity to introduce somebody to a wonderful product or service. You know that you and your team can help anyone that engages with you, so be confident in this knowledge and go and help them learn how.

- If you accept your responsibility for sales, and need help getting started, create a 100–day sales action plan and stick to it. On days you feel overwhelmed, remember to stay safely in your "three-foot world," and make just a few small steps toward your goal each day. When you wake up tomorrow, repeat the process, one day and one relentless step at a time.

- The small business owner who hires a salesperson before the company has reached the breakeven point will likely be firing that same salesperson in 30–90 days, and will have lost the same amount of time and opportunity perfecting their own sales skills. Your position as the owner or team leader will provide your prospects with a refreshing break from the professional salespeople they have to deal with each day. What a great opportunity to learn valuable sales skills; don't let it pass you by!

BOLDskill 10

Lay the groundwork for the profitable future sale of your business or division

Something is only worth what someone is willing to pay for it.
—PUBLILIUS SYRUS FROM THE 1ST CENTURY B.C.

Remember my story about Louie? Although many of the restaurants that Louie signed up for us were unaware of the extent of their contractual obligations, our airline partners loved our suddenly-larger dining program. Who doesn't like dining out at lots of great restaurants and getting airline bonus miles? The dining program became a marketplace sensation, and our competitors keenly felt our presence. My team and I often laughed together after hours as we recalled Louie's "check-writing limo tour," and raised a glass of beer as a toast to "destroying our competitors."

A few months later, with our restaurant program growing and more airlines signing on, we came into work one day and found our Sr. Product VP had "moved on to another opportunity." The rumors began to swirl and we didn't know what to think was happening. A few days later, our company's senior executive team called my division together.

"I've got great news. We're in negotiations to sell the dining program product division to our largest marketplace competitor," they announced. "And we want you to stay and help us get this done."

This was a huge lesson for me in reframing how I thought of my role as a loyal employee. We had been a subsidiary company of General Electric, and what became clear that day was that GE, like any big corporation, looks at their companies and products as assets, not as lifetime careers for their people. Our largest competitor saw the potential of combining our two dining programs together, and made an offer to purchase our division. That offer was tentatively accepted by our division CEO, pending an appropriate business asset discovery phase. We had succeeded in creating a growing GE asset, and GE had decided to convert that asset into its present value cash equivalent. For each of us that were entrusted by the company to manage a team of people and achieve our business objectives, we had helped GE win. For those who agreed to stay and work to assure that the business acquisition went successfully, it also paid off big.

Mergers and acquisitions are the name of the game

As my experience taught me, it doesn't matter if you work internally in a company or you own your own firm. The lesson here is that you should always be looking out for an exit ramp to paradise, however you define it. Once you and your team are surging, it's entirely possible that you can make yourselves valuable for a buy-out.

It happens all the time within corporate America. If you work on a corporate team, perhaps it's already happened to you. If it hasn't, it could . . . if you learn to create a Surging Team as I have taught you. If you handle yourself right and keep your perspective, you can win big.

As we made our way through the transition of ownership, our objective was no longer to grow our business—it was to assure that our business, and its intellectual property, transferred successfully to the new corporate owner. Team leaders that can calmly facilitate the transfer of company assets, when involved in a merger or acquisition, can maximize the value of the asset and realize potential financial incentives for themselves, as well as for their critical team members. I was prepared for a calm asset transfer and to cooperate with what needed to get done. However, some of my executive colleagues were completely unprepared for this change in our objectives. They did not understand or could not embrace the reality that we were now part of an intellectual property transfer process to another corporation.

Executives who are prepared for this "asset sale" event have a once-in-a-career opportunity to profit from their new objectives. During a business merger/acquisition, both the old and the new company owners need you to use all your talents and energy to transfer the intellectual property of your division to the new owners. If you can make the mental transition and accept your new objectives in the same spirit that you executed your former objectives, you will likely have the opportunity to earn a lucrative severance package, and even perhaps a transitional "stay" bonus. You may also be offered an executive position with the new owners—which might include stock options to sweeten the deal. I saw the potential for myself and decided to embrace it for the maximum compensation opportunity.

However, some of my executive colleagues could not emotionally make the transition. We now worked for a new company—the one that was buying our division. Our jobs were either temporary—through the end of the transition, or we could be hired after the transition if we demonstrated our value to the new owners. Although it was unstated, it became clear that if we impeded the transition—we would be fired. After being interviewed by my new colleagues, I was placed in charge of the business operations and technology transition, and I was soon to find out what that meant.

"We need you to fire James," said my counterpart at the new company, after coming into my office one day and closing the door.

"Why? What happened?" I asked.

"During a transition meeting yesterday, he refused to provide us the P&L financial information we requested. He told us that the requested information was 'confidential.' He doesn't realize that he works for us now, and he upset the new CFO."

"I see," I said, "I'll take care of it."

Now I liked James, but it wasn't my responsibility to be everyone's "merger psychologist." The new CFO had selected James as an example to the rest of us newly acquired human intellectual property assets. They needed our enthusiastic cooperation in order to efficiently transition and assimilate their new business. So I had to do it, as much as I was sad to see him go. He just didn't understand the transition.

I already had a big severance package with my former company, but I was then offered a package to stay, enough to hold me through the business transition. Eventually, my new company offered me an executive position after the transition that included stock options. It was a very lucrative year for me, and some of my colleagues had the same opportunity—but they rejected it. They did not want to lay the groundwork for this profitable sale of their division. They still wanted their old job with the old social network—but that job and social network were gone. Out of three "key intellectual property executives," I was the only one who was willing to make the transition to the new company. My other two colleagues declined, and likely left significant merger & acquisition opportunities on the table.

If you think that by remaining loyal to your old company, and refusing to fully cooperate in a corporate acquisition, you'll endear yourself to your friends at your old company—you are sadly wrong. There's a big difference between friends and acquaintances, and you will find (if you haven't already) that most people you work with and consider your friends, are really acquaintances, and those relationships quickly fade after you leave a company. So don't get hung up on the loyalty urge; do what's best for your own economic situation, as long as it's ethical. Fully embrace the change and move on; the sooner you do, the better for everyone. Think of yourself as a traded professional athlete—they don't look back; they only look forward to putting the money in the bank.

Never say never about selling your business

Selling your business is not an event you can always predict, but it should be one you're always prepared to consider. You'll make better foundational decisions at the startup of your business if you view it through the filter of "one day you'll want to sell it." Viewing your company through this lens will help you choose critical staff members, negotiate better employment deals with them, draft a higher quality business plan, keep better records, negotiate and maintain strong contractual agreements with clients, and get to breakeven and profitability faster. The market valuation of a profitable business is an order of magnitude greater than the valuation you can expect for a business that isn't generating sufficient profits to pay the owner fairly. Just viewing your business through this possible eventual sales filter will also compel you to run it and make decisions in a more focused way that increases its profitability and market valuation.

Years later, when I was a franchise business owner, many of my franchise owner colleagues did not embrace the premise of the BOLDskill being taught in this chapter. Some of my colleagues formed an emotional attachment to their business, to their employees, or to both—and this clouded their judgment when they were faced with critical decisions inside the crucible of running a small business. The fact is, we were each growing a personal asset by running a small business. The way to most effectively increase the value of a business asset is to run it from Day One with the understanding that as it grows in value, it will potentially bring you more cash when the time is right to sell it.

Regardless whether you intend to sell your company or not, you always need to take reasonable steps correlated with increasing your company's market value, not decreasing it. For example, both potential lenders and buyers know that a company with a team working from a formal business plan is more likely to resist distractions, overcome obstacles, and continue working toward achievement of the plan's objectives.

THE BOLD EMPLOYMENT REALITY PRINCIPLE

Six years after our dining division merger, I came face-to-face with what I call the BOLD Employment Reality Principle. By modifying the famous "Peter Principle" to accommodate the market realities of today's economy, the BOLD Employment Reality Principle states:

"In today's organizations, one will rise to his level of incompetence, or one's compensation will eventually rise beyond the organization's salary threshold. After rising to either point, you're more likely to be fired, but that opens the door to your next opportunity."

I believe that this is how the business world works today. Organizations have a threshold for incompetence, but they also have one for compensation. When you rise to a point on either scale, you risk losing your job—but this is yet another opportunity for anyone with the presence of mind and the courage to seize it.

After the acquisition of our unit at GE, I remained with my "merged" employer for 6 years and was successful. By then, however, I found that my career had run its most lucrative course, and

It's important to note that you don't usually get to choose when the time is right to sell your small business for its maximum value. When someone else believes the time is right to purchase your business or division, that's usually the first signal that you've achieved your objective and that your asset has grown enough to be recognized and valued by someone who has the means and vision to buy it. If you're prepared to seize this opportunity, you can maximize your financial gain, and you owe it to yourself and to your family to consider doing so.

Remember our BOLD Success Principle: "Success follows a predictable course. It's not the brightest who succeed, or those presented with a perfect opportunity. Success follows those who have

---

my new employer seemed to agree that they could no longer pay me the compensation I'd grown accustomed to. They offered me (politely) a chance to leave—and I took it.

I saw this event not as a failure, but as an incredible opportunity to do something completely different with my life. After researching some options, I decided to purchase a franchise business. Using the same BOLDskill of "laying the groundwork for the profitable, future sale of your business or division," I was able to run and grow my franchise business, making a six-figure annual income each year, and then I sold it profitably after eight years. In fact, without the recent experience of profitably selling my franchise business, this book would be incomplete and maybe even naïve.

The moral of my story here is: Don't be afraid of selling your business or of undergoing a corporate merger or acquisition. Make BOLD decisions to make great use of whatever opportunities come your way. Don't look back at where you were or you will miss the road ahead.

been given ordinary opportunities—and who have the presence of mind and the courage to seize them."

Whether you're leading a corporate unit or you own your own company, if you have the presence of mind from the start of your business to lay the groundwork for the profitable, future sale of your business or division, you will maximize your personal financial gain. That's what working is ultimately about—trading our labor and talents for financial gain. Learning this BOLDskill will maximize your gain.

Negotiating for your future business sale

When I owned my IT franchise, we once had a professional business acquisitions expert make a presentation to our top franchise owner peer-collaboration group about how to sell their businesses. He related the various, and most-likely, buy-out scenarios for the franchisees to our collaboration group. One scenario he didn't include was the most lucrative and fair scenario for the business owner—which starts with a recommendation I made previously in BOLDskill #6—hiring someone right from the start who has the motivation and talent to buy you out one day. That was how I architected my business sale. I sold on terms that were fairer to me than any terms that the expert mentioned in that meeting.

Here's how it happened. My wife and I were at one of those big recreational vehicle (RV) shows when I answered a phone call from a key team member. It was just a regular Sunday in 2013. We had been dreaming of having a new toy "someday" so we could take some trips and get away from the day-to-day pressure of running a 24/7 service company. But in an instant, that call changed my mood and my life. I saw my company flash before my eyes, crashing and burning. The key team member on the phone was considering leaving my company, and going to work with an employee I'd recently fired, whom he'd come to like as a friend.

"Hi Scott. It's Joe. I have to tell you something. Burt offered me a job and I'm thinking about taking it. Maybe we can work out a deal so I can still provide service support for you."

Joe was my top-notch service technician, who'd been with me for years. We'd negotiated some buy-out terms when he was first hired, and I thought he'd be the guy who would eventually purchase my business. Now he was telling me that he wanted to leave and join an employee whom I had let go.

I told Joe that I'd call him back, and I tried hard to enjoy the rest of the RV exhibits, but my heart and soul were no longer interested in the RVs on display. I felt anxious and fearful. I thought through possible responses to this shocking announcement from my key staff member. I searched my mind for what I was taught in business school and what I learned as a vice president for a major company to address my dilemma. None of the responses I had been taught made sense—except for one.

A couple of books I read when I was in graduate school immediately came to mind: *Getting to Yes*, by Roger Fisher and William Ury, and *You Can Negotiate Anything* by Herb Cohen. I realized I was in a negotiation scenario that would change the direction of my work and my life, and I didn't have much time to help sway the outcome.

It was late on Sunday night when we got home from the show, but I got right to work on my win-win negotiation strategy with this key employee. My mood toward the negotiation began as anxious and fearful. This soon changed to being excited when I realized I had already negotiated for significant leverage with this staff member, and it was time to invoke our initial hiring bargain: Joe had the right of first offer when I was ready to sell my business—and it was now clear that the time had just arrived. Using this already-negotiated leverage, I was confident that I could steer the outcome to a win-win.

That is the power of win-win negotiation—it empowers you, frees you from fear, and gives you an opportunity to negotiate anything to benefit both parties. But, first you have to recognize you're in a win-win negotiating scenario. If you let fear and anxiety negotiate for you, the result is usually a win-lose—and you are the loser.

My business was still operating short of the franchise company's coveted Million Dollar Annual Sales goal. I knew we needed something sublime to get us over the tipping point, but that something had to be huge. It had eluded me for the past two years. We were pretty darn close, as we had revenue gains in each of the last eight years, but we seemed to have slowed our growth trajectory. Was I growing complacent with just achieving revenue growth? The financial pressures of hiring and maintaining the staffing and client base we had, while being paid a fair salary as the owner, were certainly major factors in my planning what to do. I didn't want to do anything that would require that I reduce my own hard-earned and fair compensation, in order to keep growing the company to the million dollar mark, yet I should have realized this was a symptom of my own creeping complacency and fearfulness.

The current situation with my key employee was one that I didn't initiate, but I now recognized it as a win-win negotiating opportunity that had the power to jolt me out of complacency and seize a BOLD opportunity to achieve that Million Dollar Sales goal. You don't always get to determine when a negotiation begins; you just need to be ready to recognize it, put it into a win-win perspective, and have the courage to believe you can make it work.

It turned out that the key to achieving the Million Dollar Annual Revenue goal was something that was right in front of me, and I just didn't see it—until now. I had to be literally knocked out of my short-lived complacency, and challenged with losing a key staff member and possibly some key clients, before I recognized that the answer and opportunity was always right in front of me. Like Dorothy in the Wizard of Oz recognizing she had the power all along to leave Oz and get back to Kansas, I got to work and crafted the ultimate bonus plan for my key staff member, and sent it to him before the end of that same Sunday night.

72 Hours later . . . I got a call from Joe. He said simply, "My attorney looked it over, and it looks good. I'll sign it and send it over in a few minutes." We had just negotiated the timeline for the sale of my business to him. It was simple and had two parts:

Each quarter we were on track to hit a million in annual sales, my key employee would receive a significant cash bonus and I guaranteed the first bonus, which met his current financial needs. This jeopardized my own compensation, but I was now acting boldly in the face of that fear.

1. We agreed on the timeframe for the sale to my key employee, which was set to occur after we hit our million dollar sales goal. Now there would be two of us focused on this lofty goal, and if we achieved it, my company's valuation would be higher.

2. Stress from this episode likely caused the reappearance of an annoying eye twitch, and induced some phantom chest pains, but the crisis of Joe leaving was averted and a major win-win opportunity was put in play.

I now had a newly recharged staff member who had a powerful vested interest in achieving our financial goals. This deal was much more attractive to my key staff member than going to work for someone else, and he was more engaged than ever. Did I do the right thing by rewarding this staff member for upsetting my life and demanding my full attention? According to the principles of win-win negotiation, I had crafted a creative solution where we both achieved valued outcomes—so the answer is, YES!

Although no other members of my board of advisors (my wife and my best friend) agreed with me at the time, as the company president, I felt strongly that I had to do what I was being paid to do—lead my company to success, even if it meant that it got a new start without me. My personal advisors trusted me enough to support my decision.

With the game now set, I felt we had our best chance to achieve the Million Dollar Annual Revenue goal. The possible and profitable sale of my business was also underway, and my key staff member was 100% committed to both goals. I put my head down and charged into our end-game with everything I had in me. We were both going to go out big winners if this deal worked—however, I could also end up a big loser if my key employee were to leave after his guaranteed first bonus payment, or he wasn't serious about owning the business, or we miserably failed at growing the company over the next year.

I didn't fault my key staff member for wanting to increase his income and better provide for his family, but I knew that the opportunity I was now offering him was the best deal for both of us—a once in a lifetime deal for each of us. After all, employment in America is "employment at will." The only way to keep key people working for your company is to continue to create compelling reasons for them to stay, while retaining control of your business and remaining on track to achieve profitable performance beyond breakeven.

It's easy to give away a business; in fact, it's about as easy to do as running a business unprofitably. It's much harder to run a growing business, achieve breakeven, and sell it for close to its market valuation—as a capstone entrepreneurial event. Some people will tell you it can't be done, and they are very convincing when they talk to you. It takes almost irrational confidence in yourself to avoid their advice, and boldly advance with the success goals that you set for yourself at the start of your business adventure.

The gamble seemed fitting for this BOLD adventure, my end game was set, and in the end, we both won.

BOLD takeaways

- Selling your business is not an event you can always predict, but it should be one you're always prepared for.

- Whether you're leading a corporate unit, or whether you own your company, if you have the presence of mind from Day One to lay the groundwork for the profitable future sale of your business or division, you will maximize your potential personal financial gain. That's what working is ultimately about—trading your labor and talents for financial gain.

- A Surging Team is led by someone who is setting goals and directing his team to take actions that will ultimately increase the market valuation of his company or division. Always consider if your action as a team leader serves to increase the value of your company or department.

- Every division of a company is potentially an asset that can be sold, and the executives who work in those divisions are stewards of that asset. Team leaders who can calmly facilitate the transfer of company assets, when involved in a merger or acquisition, can maximize the value of the asset and realize the potential financial incentives for themselves as well as for critical team members.

- If you've practiced your win-win negotiation skills, and mastered the BOLD Success Principle, you are positioned to win big during a merger, acquisition, or business sale. Executives who can remain calm and focused during these delicate transactions are rewarded for their efforts.

Transforming Your Business or Corporate Unit into a Surging Team

> Great people are those who make others
> feel that they, too, can become great.
> — MARK TWAIN

Not long after winning the "Chairman's Challenge Award for Outstanding Intrapreneurship" when I was working for GE, I got a call from our Director of Human Resources, asking to see me right away. I had developed a reputation for "asking for forgiveness, not permission," so I assumed that I was about to be forgiven one more time.

After sitting down in her office, the HR Director said, "What's going on in your department, Scott?"

Not sure what she meant, I tried to buy some time, "I'm sorry, but I'm not sure what you are referring to."

"Why are so many people coming down here and asking me how to get hired into your department?" She was serious. I didn't know how to answer that question, but before I could think of something pithy, she smiled and said, "Nice job, Scott."

I had created a Surging Team, and it was impossible not to notice or want to be a part of it.

Throughout my corporate career and then into my franchise business ownership, I've repeatedly been able to create Surging Teams that work together and achieve remarkable goals. A Surging Team has increased team member happiness, higher productivity, and fewer turnovers. Along the way, I realized this was not the norm. Most companies do not create a Surging Team environment for their employees—but those that do will win almost every time in the marketplace.

I'm passionate today about creating a reliably repeatable team success system that company owners and corporate team leaders can use to quickly help their teams become happier, more productive, and unstoppable. This book has outlined for you a reliably repeatable team success system that we call the BOLDskills for Accelerated Team Success.

Here is a summary of the BOLDskills you have learned:

BOLDskill 1: Learn and then adopt the BOLD Success Principle

a. "Success follows a predictable course. It's not the brightest who succeed, or those presented with a perfect opportunity. Success follows those who have been given *ordinary* opportunities—and who have the presence of mind *and the courage* to seize them."

b. Your responsibility as a leader is to identify and have the courage to seize opportunities for your team to develop its success potential.

c. Take Dr. Martin Seligman's VIA character strengths survey to discover your signature character strengths. You can find a link to it on our website, www.boldbreak.com/take-the-via-survey. We also recommend you offer it to your team members to take as well.

d. When you, as the team leader, are aware of your own "signature strengths," and you learn to use those strengths, you'll be happier and better able to recognize and seize opportunities for your team.

BOLDskill 2: Always use a formal business plan and include your team in the process

a. Your formal business plan outlines your strategy for the evolutionary growth of your company.

b. When confronted with fear and doubt, it will be your business plan that keeps you working toward the success goals you carefully outlined.

c. Be sure to use the "likely case" and not the "best case" as the basis for the many projections in your business plan.

d. A business plan increases the value of your company in the eyes of potential buyers.

BOLDskill 3: Identify and adopt a BOLD purpose

a. You and your team's passionate belief in your company's BOLD Purpose will be communicated and put to use as a competitive advantage in the marketplace.

b. As your team faces success obstacles that require time and talent beyond their comfort zones, it will be your team's BOLD purpose that helps them look past the immediate discomfort and see the BOLD purpose you are all working toward.

c. A BOLD purpose allows each team member to connect their individual efforts with a larger and more important company purpose. It facilitates a feeling of ownership engagement among the team members.

d. You should also have a personal BOLD purpose that motivates and inspires your personal life.

> BOLDskill 4: Provide ownership engagement,
> inspired leadership, and trusted management

a. You as the company owner and team leader must provide intentional group governance role development, or your team will invent their own governance without you. The group governance roles are engaged ownership, inspired leadership, and trusted management.

b. In order to inspire their best performances, you as the team leader need to provide opportunities for your team members to feel the kind of engagement in their work that owners feel. That is done by selecting and promoting your team's BOLD purpose, one that your team members can identify with.

c. Your team deserves inspired leadership, someone they will follow when things are uncertain. If you don't provide inspired leadership, someone on your team will, because your team members will seek it.

d. Trust is hard to earn, easy to lose, and almost impossible to get back. Your team needs to trust that they will be treated fairly. Use objective, not subjective, metrics to measure team and individual progress toward their goals.

> BOLDskill 5: BOLDLY work to increase
> your team's positive collective spirit

a. A team leader that develops the key team elements will set the conditions for a positive collective spirit to emerge. The five key team elements are: goal urgency, BOLD purpose, clear accountability, increasing team member well-being, and entrepreneurial collaboration.

b. When confronted with a success obstacle, a Surging Team can source innovative ideas which the team leader can decide to deploy in order to get past the obstacle and on to success. This is the development of revolutionary change potential.

c. Continually achieving team goals increases a team's success potential—eventually creating a feeling that they'll always win.

d. Every team member deserves a leader who is working to increase their individual feelings of happiness and well-being, while striving to achieve their BOLD purpose. Do you know your team member's signature character strengths, and how to leverage them?

BOLDskill 6: Hire or fire according to strategic goals, not out of panic or convenience

a. Your team members deserve to work with people who have the talent and the energy to achieve the team's success goals.

b. It's easy to continue and add people to your team, and much harder to reevaluate the real needs of the team—in the face of their current goals—while staying within your budget.

c. Be alert and willing to make changes in team composition and in the roles of the team members. Consciously and creatively find ways to keep salary costs contained. When you do need to hire someone, you'll have the budget and the reputation to get approval for the hire. Try to promote from within to earn the trust of your team. Be vigilant for team members who quit, but fail to tell you.

d. Firing team members is inevitable, and the quicker the termination cycle is completed, the better for everyone on your team. Be vigilant for team members who quit, but fail to tell you.

e. Use a standardized employment personality test—and believe the results you get! Don't discount that people can be crazy or disruptive to your team if the survey indicates even minor oddities in their behavior.

BOLDskill 7: Practice win-win negotiation in all spheres of your business relationships

a. Nobody wants to feel that they lost in a negotiation, and that is the power of win-win negotiation—there is no loser.

b. Awareness of negotiating opportunities with employees, clients, team members, peers, and family is the beginning of win-win negotiation.

c. You as the team leader must master win-win negotiation in order to develop an unstoppable Surging Team. It is one of the most important BOLDskills.

BOLDskill 8: Make peace with fear and doubt

a. Be sure you have a well-crafted business plan to rely on when you're feeling fear and doubt.

b. If you're feeling afraid, you likely are imagining the worst case scenario. Learn to argue with yourself and to rationally evaluate a more likely outcome to the current issue that is causing your fears.

c. "Stay in your three-foot world" and just move one handhold forward each day toward your success goals. Sometimes thinking of the big picture can be immobilizing, so you must pull yourself back to stay in your three-foot world.

d. Maintain an exercise program and time for meditation or prayer to rest your mind.

e. Take a vacation now and then to relax and clear your mind.

BOLDskill 9: Become a BOLD salesperson for your business and your team

a. You can't outsell your mindset, so if you think you can't sell, you won't be able to. A negative attitude about sales becomes a self-fulfilling prophecy.

b. If your team is not critical in supporting the sales process, then your team will likely be one of the first that's asked to reduce staff during the next company budget cycle.

c. Find a way to help your team get involved with sales. Sales are the only way to achieve success in business, so find opportunities for your team to assist the company's sales team.

d. Clients and prospects enjoy talking to non-sales professionals, so take advantage of that, but let your clients and prospects do most of the talking!

e. It's the salesperson who owns the client relationship, so be sure that your clients see you as the chief salesperson and owner.

BOLDskill 10: Lay the groundwork for the profitable future sale of your business or division

a. If you own your own company:
  - Run it as if you'll be selling it one day soon. This mindset helps you restrict yourself to doing things that increase the value of your company.
  - Set yourself up, from Day One, to be able to take advantage of all potential avenues to sell your company in the future. Hiring a key employee who has the desire to buy the company from you is a strategic move that could bring you the highest value.

b. If you work for a corporation, act as if it's your responsibility to increase the value of your corporate department.

c. Keep your team's compensation costs down.

d. Recognize that you will be seen as the holder of valuable intellectual property for your corporation.

e. If there is an acquisition of your division, you could come away a big winner if you can keep your perspective.

f. You don't usually get to choose when someone else decides that your company or division has value as an acquisition to them, so work to increase that value. Be open when an opportunity comes along. If you keep your perspective during an acquisition, you can come away a big winner.

g. The sale of your business or the acquisition of your division will challenge your win-win negotiating skills. Take advantage of negotiating opportunities so you have lots of practice, and are ready when the sale or acquisition happens.

Your success at creating a Surging Team takes courage to accept risk and danger

We're all fascinated by people who have lives filled with danger and risk taking—especially when they're in pursuit of a worthy, BOLD and seemingly impossible goal. We never tire of seeing how people creatively overcome obstacles and achieve things "that couldn't be done." As my mother was maddeningly fond of repeating to me:

> *Somebody said that it couldn't be done, but he with a*
> *chuckle replied, 'Maybe it couldn't, but he would be one*
> *that wouldn't say so until he'd tried . . .*
> — *Edgar Guest, from the poem "It Couldn't Be Done"*

As a leader, developing higher productivity and happiness among your team members is one of the most worthy goals you can work towards—and, if you succeed, you will increase your company's profitability. Be BOLD, seize this opportunity, and start applying the BOLDskills for Accelerated Team Success in your business, even when others aren't yet behind you and some even doubt that you will succeed. As General Patton once said (which my son who is now a United States Marine can relate to): "Lead, follow, or get out of the way."

We all dream of facing and overcoming danger, and we all want success in our professional and personal lives. Business failures deeply affect us, and increase the risk of relational problems and even divorce. When I started my franchise business, my life was far from perfect. My marriage had become strained from too many corporate business trips to distant cities. My children were growing up with me away on business most of the week, and I feared for both my career and my family. I set a goal to do something risky and dangerous, with the BOLD Purpose of achieving work-life balance, so that I could be there for my young family during a critical and unrepeatable time. I thought that by starting my own business, I could achieve this balance. Nine years later, I wrote in my personal journal:

> As my wife and I proudly watched our son and his Marine Corps boot camp company receive their titles as United States Marines, I wondered if this would have been possible if I hadn't achieved work-life balance and had the personal vision and availability to be there with my family and help my wife raise our children during these last few years. I wanted to be there and actively help to keep my kids from getting lost in the many temptations of this world, and not be far away on business, in opaque places, while they wandered without me. I looked around, and my family was all

sitting here now. My wife and I were celebrating the achievement of our son, and my children were all here too, honoring their "little brother," and each of them now a successful and flourishing young adult. I thanked God for the opportunity to be there for them, and the courage to recognize and seize the opportunity.

Looking back, it was again the development of a Surging Team in my franchise business that brought us over the finish line. Our Surging Team environment allowed me to distribute critical work responsibilities and create fulfilling jobs for my team—jobs that allowed them to flourish and allowed me to craft a professional and a personal work-life balance. Our Surging Company also provided the opportunity for my wife to join me in the drive to achieve success beyond what I had ever imagined.

This is what I want for you, the team leader, the company owner, the reader of this book. I want you to look back with no regrets and know that you tackled the things that seemingly couldn't be done—succeed in both your business and in your personal life—through the development of an unstoppable Surging Team to stand behind you, and with you.

I hope I have provided you with some inspiring real-life examples to motivate you, and that the hard-fought, work-life success principles that are embodied in our BOLDskills for Accelerated Team Success training will help you set up the conditions to achieve astounding, repeatable success, both on your own team and in your own life. Along my journey, I have learned that sometimes just knowing that someone else understands the magnitude of your struggle, is enough to keep you in the fight. Other times, you need a new strategy or tactic to launch you past seemingly impossible barriers. This book provides you with both.

Now, go seize your Team's future and lead them in an unstoppable Surge!

APPENDICES

Appendix A:
The BOLDskills for Accelerated Team Success
Training Mini Reminder

Photocopy this page and keep it in front of you as a reminder of the power you can achieve when you decide to commit yourself to becoming the leader of an unstoppable Surging Team.

Our BOLD Purpose at BOLDbreak, Inc.

We provide leaders the tools to create unstoppable Surging Teams inside their company or department.

Why is it important to create Surging Teams?

Surging teams always achieve their objectives, on time and within budget, which allows a company to meet their goals. Members of Surging Team have higher levels of productivity, report higher levels of well-being, have lower turn-over, have better health and increase the profitability of their company.

What are the characteristics of a Surging Team?

- Is made up of ordinary people, with a shared Noble Purpose
- Has a leader that they trust
- Believes they'll always win, and are permanently imprinted by success

- Innovates ways around all internal and external obstacles and refuses to give up.
- Always meets their objectives, on time and within budget

What is the responsibility of the team leader?

The leader of a company or a department is responsible for creating a successful team that can achieve company objectives. By mastering the BOLDskills for Accelerated Team Success, a team leader is equipped to nurture and create the conditions for an unstoppable Surging Team to emerge.

What is BOLDskills for Accelerated Team Success Training?

BOLDskills for Accelerated Team Success Training is a reliably repeatable training program that provides leaders the tools to nurture the conditions that allow a Surging Team to emerge.

These are the 10 BOLDskills that every leader of a Surging Team must master:

1. Learn and then adopt the BOLD Success Principle
2. Always use a formal business plan and include your team in the process
3. Identify and adopt a BOLD purpose
4. Provide ownership engagement, inspired leadership, and trusted management
5. BOLDLY work to increase the positive spirit of your team
6. Hire or fire according to strategic goals, not out of panic or convenience
7. Practice win-win negotiation in all spheres of your business relationships
8. Make peace with fear and doubt; they are constant companions of leaders
9. Become a BOLD salesperson for your business and your team
10. Lay the groundwork for the profitable future sale of your business or division

Appendix B: Signature Strengths Org Chart
Copy this page as many times as needed.

Team Leader:	Team Member:
Strength 1:	
Strength 2:	
Strength 3:	
Strength 4:	
Strength 5:	

Team Leader:	Team Member:
Strength 1:	
Strength 2:	
Strength 3:	
Strength 4:	
Strength 5:	

Team Leader:	Team Member:
Strength 1:	
Strength 2:	
Strength 3:	
Strength 4:	
Strength 5:	

Team Leader:	Team Member:
Strength 1:	
Strength 2:	
Strength 3:	
Strength 4:	
Strength 5:	

Appendix C: BOLDskills for Accelerated Team Success— Team Leader Self-Assessment

Take this self-assessment to identify which BOLDskills you need to work on. Place an 'X' in the box that best describes your current proficiency level with each of the critical entrepreneurship success skills.

	The Critical Team BOLDskills	Lacking	Improving	Proficient	Expert
1.	Learn and then adopt the BOLD Success Principle				
2.	Always use a formal business plan and include your team in the process				
3.	Identify and Adopt a BOLD purpose				
4.	Provide ownership engagement, inspired leadership and trusted management				
5.	BOLDLY work to increase the positive collective spirit of your team				
6.	Hire or fire according to strategic goals, not out of panic or convenience				
7.	Practice win-win negotiation in all spheres of your business relationships				
8.	Make peace with fear and doubt; they are the constant companions of leaders				
9.	Become a BOLD salesperson for your business, and your team				
10.	Lay groundwork for the profitable, future sale of your business or division				
	Total number in each category				

Appendix D: The Surging Team Profile Assessment

Would you describe your company or your corporate team as a Surging Team?

Take this assessment to gauge your team's Surging Team Success profile. If you are the team leader, answer the questions for yourself as a team member. It was also designed to be taken by each team member, so offer it to them, too.

If your "Yes" scores are greater than your "No" scores, then your team is on the way to becoming an unstoppable Surging Team. If your team has at least 11 "Yes" scores, then your team is displaying multiple Surging Team characteristics and your team leader is doing a good job. As the company owner or team leader, your goal is to improve the combined Surging Team profile "Yes," scores of your team members, and we can help you can get there!

	Surging Team Profile Assessment Questions	No	Maybe	Yes
1.	Does each member of your team understand what their shared BOLD purpose is?			
2.	Do you trust your direct team leader, whether it's the business owner, or another executive?			
3.	Do you believe that your team will overcome all obstacles and eventually succeed?			
4.	Has your team innovated creative ways to get around problems and obstacles?			
5.	Is each team member included in the planning process to set the team's objectives?			
6.	Does your team always achieve its objectives?			
7.	Does your team leader ask for and implement ideas proposed by the team members?			
8.	Do you feel that there is a direct link between your individual efforts on the team, and the success of the team?			

9.	Are your team members able to overcome the drama in their lives, so they can work effectively?			
10.	Is your team leader effective in resolving both internal and external conflict that impedes your team's success?			
11.	Is quitting your job unimaginable?			
12.	Have you experienced extended periods of engagement, or "being in the flow" while working?			
13.	Do you feel a powerfully positive collective spirit when your team is together?			
14.	Does your team have stories they tell that demonstrate their positive collective spirit, vand its BOLD purpose?			
15.	Is your company achieving high levels of profitability?			
	Total number in each category			

You can also use feedback from these two additional questions in your assessment:

- Describe how it feels to be part of your team:

- What would help your team perform better?

Appendix E: The Surging Team Strength Gap Analysis

When evaluating a potential team success opportunity, use the following chart to determine which signature strengths your team members collectively possess, and how these combined strengths may influence you to either seize a success opportunity for your team, or if you have the option—to let the opportunity pass.

Description

One exercise to evaluate an opportunity, is to prepare a diagram showing "where we are" on one side of the diagram, and "where the opportunity could take us" on the other side—and the gap in the middle is where we need to explore "building a bridge using the team's character strengths" to succeed in the opportunity. Have your Signature Strengths Org Chart from Appendix B completed and in front of you. Now imagine several character strengths that could be leveraged to build the bridge and achieve the success outcome for a given opportunity. You can engage your team to help in this bridge-building exercise. The objective with this exercise is to be aware of what strengths will be needed and then making an informed decision on whether those strengths are present in enough quantity on your team to achieve the objectives represented by this opportunity.

- What is the opportunity being evaluated?

- Why does your company want to achieve the objectives represented by this opportunity?

- Where is your team now in being able to achieve the objectives represented by this opportunity?

- Which of the signature character strengths could be used to build a bridge between where your company is now, and where it needs to be, in order to achieve the objectives represented by this opportunity? Choose several character strengths that could be used to build a bridge, using the Surging Team Strength Gap Analysis chart below:

SURGING TEAM STRENGTH GAP ANALYSIS

Character Strengths	How could this character strength be used to achieve the objectives represented by this opportunity?	Which team members have this as one of their signature strengths?
Creativity		
Curiosity		
Judgment		
Love of Learning		
Perspective		
Bravery		
Perseverance		
Honesty		
Zest		
Love		
Kindness		
Social Intelligence		
Teamwork		
Fairness		
Leadership		
Forgiveness		
Humility		
Prudence		
Self-Regulation		
Appreciation of Beauty and Excellence		
Gratitude		
Hope		
Humor		
Spirituality		

Appendix F: ABCDE Exercise for
Identifying and Overcoming Fear

This exercise is designed to help you "argue with yourself" and change your habitual beliefs that follow fears you have. If you can change those habitual beliefs to better reflect accuracy, then your reaction to your current and future fears will change to better reflect a more accurate view. Your goal is to become skilled at undoing a damaging personal fear habit by becoming skilled at generating alternative, and more accurate, beliefs about your fears.

ABCDE Component	Your Descriptions
Adversity	What is the fear you have encountered? Write in the space on the next page a description of what is happening, not your evaluation of it. Be objective and don't make inferences (client x is probably going to cancel our agreement) but instead record a fact (client x was unhappy). You can record your inference in the "belief" section.
Belief	Your belief is how you interpret the above fear. What is your initial thought about this fear, your immediate belief? How does it affect your team's objectives?
Consequences	Record your feelings, and any actions you took or plan to take as a result of your belief. Include as many feelings and actions as you can recall (i.e. "I promised a lower price," "I spent the rest of the day terrified," "I was unable to work," "I declined the opportunity," "I accepted a revised delivery date.")
Dispute	Your reflexive beliefs may or may not be facts, and are more likely distortions and catastrophic thinking, so dispute each belief in the space below. Try to find the accuracies in each adversity (i.e. "I am blowing things out of proportion," "I know my boss still respects me and appreciates our team," "We have the talent on our team to get this done.")
Energy	How did you feel after you disputed your initial belief about your fear by using facts? Did you feel energized and free to choose other actions, and not automatically accept the usual consequences?

ABCDE Component	Your Descriptions
Adversity	
Belief	
Consequences	
Dispute	
Energy	

Appendix G: 100–day Sales Action Plan

FOR TEAMS DIRECTLY INVOLVED WITH SALES:

1.	Choose 5 sales channels from the list below, below and focus on only those sales channels for this 100 day period. Do not choose less than 5, as a multi-channel sales approach is the most effective.
2.	Decide which of your potential prospect lists (using the chart below) will be targeted by each chosen sales channel in your 100–day sales action plan.
3.	What sales outcome are you looking for during this 100 days?
	a. For example, assuming you want to achieve 6 sales during this 100 day (14 week) period, you need to get face-to-face with at least 2 prospects per week.
	b. In order to get face-to-face with at least 2 prospects per week, you need to contact 100 times this number, or 200 contacts per week and 2,800 sales contacts over the 100 day sale period.
4.	How will you achieve the above outcome, using your chosen sales channels and potential prospect lists? How many new clients do you expect from each sales channel?
5.	What are the actions that need to be taken in order to achieve those results?
6.	Who will take the actions and when, in order to achieve your expected sales results, by sales channel, during the current 100 days?
7.	What are the expenses related to the actions you've identified?
8.	Keep track of the results, by sales channel.

Here is a list of possible sales channels
for your product or service

Cold calling and dropping off a "gift" at some targeted prospects, send a direct mail piece, send a printed newsletter, send an email, send an emailed newsletter, initiate a telemarketing campaign, make list verification phone calls (just want to make sure this phone number is correct, by the way, can I get an email address?), attend networking events (BNI, LeTip, Chamber of Commerce), get an article published online or in print, start an online blog, plan an in-person seminar or webinar to discuss a trending business topic and invite people to attend, purchase Google adwords, use social media to promote your product, attend a trade show, create a video to promote your product and add this video to your website and social media, add your sales channel preferences.

POTENTIAL PROSPECT LISTS FOR YOUR 100 DAY SALES ACTION PLAN

1.	Existing clients who may purchase additional products or services
2.	Prospects who responded to a marketing campaign in the past, but did not purchase from you.
3.	Generate a new list of prospects from a list provider like INFOUSA.
4.	Ask your clients and colleagues for referrals.
5.	Ask a vendor if you can market to their clients (joint marketing).
6.	Visit several businesses that are close to your existing clients and introduce yourself.
7.	Your own prospect list ideas.

100 DAY SALES ACTION PLAN— FOR TEAMS NOT DIRECTLY INVOLVED WITH SALES

1.	Meet with colleagues who are team leaders that directly support sales, and ask them how your team can help them achieve their sales goals.
2.	Propose that you or members of your team ride-along with them on a sales call.
3.	Work to get some "sales support" activities into your team's objectives.
4.	Follow-up to make sure your team's assistance did indeed help the direct sales teams.
5.	Be sure your team is aware of the results of their sales support actions.

Appendix H: Worksheet for Exploring Additional Creative Uses of Signature Strengths

How to Practice and Better Use your Signature Character Strengths

Use this worksheet to choose from your top five signature character strengths, and brainstorm how you can practice using your strengths and then tapping into those strengths to accomplish a task. For each of the 24 possible signature character strengths, I have provided sample ideas to help you practice, but you can think of your own ideas too.

First, think of a task that requires you to use one or more of your signature strengths, and keep this in mind as you practice using your top 5 signature character strengths:

INSERT YOUR TASK HERE

Learn your signature character strengths by taking the VIA Character Survey. You can find a link to the survey on our website, www.boldbreak.com/take-the-via-survey. Here are the 24 Character Strengths as identified by the VIA Character Institute, followed by four ideas for practicing how to use this strength more often:

1. CREATIVITY
   a. Create and refine at least one original idea weekly in an area of your interest. This could be an article, a poem, a drawing or a story.
   b. Work on your assignments in a new and different environment.
   c. Look for different ways to spend more time at tasks you do best.
   d. Brainstorm with your colleagues on alternate ways to complete a challenging task.

2. CURIOSITY
   a. Make a list of unknowns about a favorite topic.
   b. When doing a task that you don't care for, notice something about the task that you never noticed before.
   c. When talking to people who drain you, consider what signature strengths likely make them act the way they do.
   d. Connect with a person of a different culture and spend time learning about their heritage.

3. JUDGMENT
   a. Identify the last 3 actions at work that you weren't happy with and consider a better alternative.
   b. Identify a time when you didn't think through your actions carefully enough and develop a method to give yourself more time to think before you act next time.
   c. When deciding about an important issue, write down the pros and cons.
   d. Imagine the best and worst case scenarios for an important challenge you or your team are facing, and use them to determine the "most likely case."

4. LOVE OF LEARNING
   a. Deliberately learn 5 new words—and use them today.
   b. Identify a topic you have expertise in and how you can share your knowledge with your peers.
   c. Read a book and maybe even get several team members to read the same book.
   d. Set a time to discuss a topic of mutual interest with a team member.

5. PERSPECTIVE
   a. Explain the broad outlook of your team's BOLD purpose in a few sentences.

     b. Read quotes of wisdom and re-write them as small practical steps for yourself

     c. Examine a major company event from its historical, economic, or ownership perspective.

     d. Seek a role that requires you to counsel others.

6. BRAVERY

     a. Resist social pressure and choose to act on noble values.

     b. Ask questions that help you and others face reality, and offer a solution.

     c. Look for stories of bravery in the news and on your own team.

     d. Establish a relationship with someone on your team who is outside your comfortable friendship profile.

7. PERSEVERANCE

     a. When does persevering feel engrossing as opposed to a chore?

     b. Set small daily or weekly goals and accomplish them on time.

     c. Reframe setbacks as challenges.

     d. Partner with someone or befriend someone on your team who is highly perseverant.

8. HONESTY

     a. Provide honest feedback when asked to provide critical input, as in a satisfaction survey.

     b. Identify an area in which you have a strong moral conviction

     c. Catch yourself telling small lies.

     d. Review the ethical standards of your profession.

9. ZEST

     a. Start an exercise routine or try a new routine. Encourage your team to also add zest into their lives.

b. Think of ways to make an assignment exciting and see if you can focus to the point when you lose track of time.

c. When your colleagues begin to laugh, notice how infectious it is.

d. Take time to celebrate your next team or individual accomplishment or victory and invite the team to celebrate with you.

10. LOVE

a. Journal about your work relationships and what is most valued in those relationships.

b. Consider if your thoughts, statements and your writings to other people are expressing loving kindness.

c. Talk to someone on the team and ask them to review some details about their day or about a recent event.

d. Be sure to celebrate important dates of your close friends, family, and co-workers.

11. KINDNESS

a. Perform 3 random acts of kindness each week.

b. Visit, write, or show kindness to someone who is not feeling well.

c. Pay for lunch.

d. Practice "giving way to others" while driving, while in a crowded place, or in a meeting when others are trying to express a thought or who need encouragement to express their thoughts.

12. SOCIAL INTELLIGENCE

a. Withhold a powerful and decisive argument that will win a discussion but might hurt someone.

b. Listen carefully to a team member and resist a rebuttal.

c. If someone offends you, think of what temporary event may be causing their offensive behavior.

d. Learn the signature character strengths of your co-workers or your family—or guess what they may be

13. TEAMWORK
   a. Set a goal that requires another person to complete part of the task.
   b. Offer to help a colleague.
   c. Decorate a community place, like a lunch area, or clean it up.
   d. Start an interest club (chess, garden, or athletic club, etc.)

14. FAIRNESS
   a. The next time you make a mistake, notice if you admit it. Do you take credit for a success, or do you share the credit with others?
   b. Encourage equal participation in the next group discussion.
   c. Consider the likely character strengths of the people in your next meeting and avoid stereotypes
   d. Read a biography of a person who exemplifies justice

15. LEADERSHIP
   a. Volunteer to lead the next discussion.
   b. Organize an event for your colleagues or family.
   c. Rotate a leadership role you already have with others to share leadership with them.
   d. Ask people you've worked with to write a testimonial of your leadership style.

16. FORGIVENESS
   a. Recall a time you were forgiven.
   b. Consider if there is someone on your team you can forgive.
   c. Ask for forgiveness from a Divine power and assess how you feel afterwards.
   d. Consider someone who holds an obvious grudge and how you feel about that person.

17. HUMILITY
    a. Identify who inspired you and write them a letter to thank them.
    b. Allow other people to notice your skills on their own without calling your skills to their attention.
    c. Notice if you speak more than the others in a group situation and consider listening more.
    d. Be aware of your place as a role model and act with that in mind.

18. PRUDENCE
    a. Perform a cost/benefit analysis.
    b. Drive more cautiously.
    c. Visualize the consequences of a decision in a 1, 5 and 10 year time frame.
    d. Practice win-win and avoid win-lose scenarios.

19. SELF-REGULATION
    a. Get enough rest and then set aside the time needed to prepare your options.
    b. When you get upset, try to find something positive about the situation or the other person
    c. Identify a few role models and consider why you chose them
    d. Deliberately fast from a comfort or a food you enjoy for a month.

20. APPRECIATION OF BEAUTY AND EXCELLENCE
    a. Is there an aspect of beauty or excellence in the issue you're facing?
    b. Add something aesthetic to your work space.
    c. Notice the excellence of someone's character strengths.
    d. Notice and appreciate someone who has done excellent work.

21. GRATITUDE
    a. Think of three blessings in your life right now.
    b. Notice how often you express gratitude and whether the sentiment is authentically felt.
    c. Leave a note for someone who has helped you.
    d. Be still for 5 minutes and consider what you are grateful for.

22. HOPE
    a. What is the best case scenario?
    b. Watch a movie that promotes a message of hope and think about how it applies to your life.
    c. Schedule at least 15 minutes twice a week for generating optimistic ideas.
    d. List a bad thing that happened at work and find a positive aspect or insight you gained.

23. HUMOR
    a. Smile and realize that no matter what results from your decision, nothing you do will change the destiny of mankind.
    b. Try to cheer up someone who seems down
    c. If you start feeling stressed, think of something funny about the situation.
    d. If you start to get upset, consider if you're taking yourself a little too seriously and poke a little fun at yourself.

24. SPIRITUALITY
    a. Reflect on the BOLD purpose of your company and think of ways that your decision fits in
    b. Look for "the sacred" in everyday experiences.
    c. Read a spiritual or religious book every day for 15 minutes.
    d. Consider which of your daily actions have lasting significance for yourself or for others—how will they remember you?

Appendix I: Team Goal-Setting Template to Achieve Accountability of Success Goals

Team leader:

Team member:

Team:

Date:

Team Success GOAL #:

Name of Goal:

Description of team success goal:

Describe Team Member Goal related to the Team Success Goal #:

How to measure team member progress on this goal:

Company resources needed by the team member to achieve the goal:

Planned Action Steps by Team member:

Deadline for Member Goal completion:

Which Team Member Signature Strengths Can Be Leveraged?

1. Summarize your progress on your individual goal. How did your progress on this individual goal affect team goal achievement?

2. If you met your goal what contributed to your success?

3. If you did not meet your goal or are falling behind schedule what are barriers to your success?

4. If you are falling behind schedule what are some ideas to help you get back ontrack for completing on time & within budget?

5. If you achieved this goal please write a brief anecdote that helps the team understand how you achieved this goal and which signature strengths you used.

Appendix J: The Surging Team Collective Spirit Worksheet

This exercise is reproduced from BOLDskill 5 and you can photocopy it and fill it out when you need to use it. It is a tool you
can use to help develop your team's positive collective spirit by
putting it to work to solve a team problem. Use this worksheet
to identify a critical team goal that's falling behind schedule, then
brainstorm to identify options to get back on schedule, choose an
option, and track progress until the goal is achieved. Have a Signature Strengths Org Chart in front of you that has the top five
strengths of each of your team members (like the one provided
in Appendix B). Remember: "A Surging Team always meets their
goals, on time and within budget."

1. What team, department, or company goals are falling behind
   schedule?

2. Rank the "falling behind schedule" goals by required completion
   date, then choose one that has the nearest completion date and/
   or the most urgency.

3. Make sure your team is aware of this goal, the completion date,
   and your budgetary constraints.

4. What metric is being used to measure progress toward this
   goal? If none, then create an appropriate metric and write it
   here.

5. What is your team's current progress toward this goal?

6. Gather your team and begin brainstorming to assure that this
   goal will be completed, on time, and within budget. Reiterate
   your team's BOLD purpose to start this brainstorming meeting and keep their individual character strengths in mind as
   the brainstorming session proceeds. Each time a team member
   offers a solution during the brainstorming session, repeat their

solution back to them, framed in the strength that's exhibited by the proposed solution (i.e., "proposing we work late demonstrates your strength of persistence").

7. From the brainstorming session, identify several potential solutions to get your team back on track to achieve the goal. Then select one of these solutions either as the team leader on behalf of your team (team leadership is not a democracy, so you can indeed choose one of the solutions), or you can involve your team in voting on the choice of a final solution.

8. Implement the solution, and agree to measure progress toward this goal at least once a week, using the agreed upon metric, and publish the metric results for the whole team to see each week.

9. Determine if your team's journey to goal attainment is a candidate for a team BOLD purpose reinforcement story (one told over and over to reinforce team collective spirit and BOLD purpose). If so, write a brief paragraph that encompasses the team victory.

Appendix K: Strategic Hiring Worksheet

		Yes	No	Maybe
1.	Are you hiring according to strategic goals?			
2.	Do new employees sign a non-compete?			
3.	Do you have a formal organization chart showing the signature character strengths of each team member (see appendix B)?			
4.	Do you have formal roles and responsibilities for each position on your organization chart?			
5.	Do you know what metrics will be used to measure goals?			
6.	Does the new position have some team goals, some company goals, and some personal goals?			
7.	Do you know how does this new position you're hiring for will increase your team's success potential?			
8.	Is there anyone currently on your team that can take on the responsibilities of the new position you intend to hire for (be certain you aren't overlooking a great internal candidate)?			
9.	Have you reviewed your team's job descriptions to determine if you can eliminate some obsolete tasks and possibly add new tasks that would allow you to avoid hiring someone right now?			
10.	If everyone on your team was performing to the level you expect, would you need to hire?			
11.	Do you have a metric you use to manage the % of company revenue spent on staff compensation?			
12.	According to this metric, are you overpaying anyone on your team?			
13.	Do you use an employment focused personality test before hiring?			
14.	Do you have several key members of your team interview job candidates?			
15.	Do you ask interviewing team members if they noticed any odd interviewee behavior?			
16.	What compensation alternatives do you have to offer, besides higher salary?			
	Totals			

Appendix L: Strategic Firing Worksheet

		Yes	No	Maybe
1.	Are you firing appropriately in order to meet your team's strategic goals?			
2.	Do you suspect that anyone on your team has "quit" but hasn't told you yet?			
3.	Do your company revenues support your current staff compensation, based on your metric?			
4.	Do you know how long you will wait before taking action to reduce staff compensation?			
5.	Do you know your options for reducing staff compensation?			
6.	Do you have a rating for how each member of your team is performing today?			
7.	Are each of your team members meeting or exceeding your expectations?			
8.	Are you planning to replace anyone who is not meeting expectations?			
9.	When you fire someone, do you pay them a severance?			
10.	If so, do the severance conditions include a reminder of their non-compete agreement?			
11.	Do you meet individually with your remaining team members after you let someone go?			
12.	Are you prepared to have your attorney send a "non-compete reminder" to the fired employee if you suspect they are attempting to sabotage?			
13.	If your weak team leaders are not improving, are you planning to replace them?			
14.	Do you have members of your team trained to handle the responsibilities of the employee to be let go?			
15.	Are you worried that if you fired a non-performing employee or team leader, that you may lose clients?			
16.	According to your compensation metric, are you working to replace any overcompensated team members?			
	Totals			

Appendix M: Win-Win Negotiation Worksheet

Complete the win-win negotiation worksheet below and list some important agreements and relationships that you need to negotiate or re-negotiate. Include situations you or your team are facing today that would benefit from win-win negotiation.

1.	What situation are you or your team facing today that could benefit from win-win negotiation?
2.	Create a list of your needs, including your bottom line, must-have need and make sure you have more than just your must-have need on the list.
3.	Is there a negotiating deadline and who has the deadline?
4.	Create a list of what you believe are the other party's needs.
5.	Identify what you think is their must-have, bottom line need.
6.	What sources of power do you have in the negotiation?
7.	What sources of power does the other party have?
8.	What is your strategy to get a win-win result?
9.	Use informal discussions with the other party to get a sense of what they'd be like as a contractual partner, kind of like "dating."
10.	Based on these informal discussions, determine if you'd want your team or your company to be bound to a contractual agreement with the other party.

Acknowledgments

I'm grateful for the opportunities I've had in my life and career so far, and want to thank:

My wife, Patty, who served on my personal board of directors, and saved our franchise business one memorable night. My children, Melissa, Joann, Carly, Kelly and Trevor, who gave me five powerful reasons to live a life of no regrets. They've each since showed me that they also learned to dare greatly in their own lives—and never surrender. Patty and I are so very proud of them.

My Mom, who responded to my numerous childhood threats to "give up" by quoting Edgar Guest's poem, "It Couldn't Be Done," in its entirety, over my exasperated objections, and so many times that I can recite the first verse by memory upon demand:

Somebody said that it couldn't be done, But he with a chuckle
replied, That 'maybe it couldn't', but he would be one,
Who wouldn't say so til he'd tried. So he buckled right in with the
trace of a grin on his face, If he worried he hid it. He started to sing as
he tackled the thing, That couldn't be done, and he did it!
—Thanks for teaching me, Mom. I love you

My Grandma Victoria and Grandpa Alex, who gave me a wild place to be a boy on their farm in South Dakota, and taught me about unconditional love.

My best friend, Sam Licari, who believed that my franchise business would succeed—before anyone else did—just because

I was running it. Day after day, Sam calmly walked me back from fear and doubt, or just listened patiently to my entrepreneurial struggles. He did this even while confronting his own fears. I can't repay you, Sam, but we can "raise up our glasses against evil forces" again soon.

The CMIT Pacesetters peer group, who passionately refused to accept the status quo, and forged a way to success; and Jeff, the CMIT franchise CEO, who relentlessly encouraged peer collaboration, and provided his franchisees a unique national forum to succeed and be recognized by their peers.

John Eldredge for his book, *Wild at Heart*, which encouraged me to dare greatly, take a bold step, and make the terrifying decision to start a business; and Lisa McLeod, for her book, *Selling with Noble Purpose*, which challenged us to find and embrace a Noble Purpose for our business, one that we could rally around when our courage was faltering.

To my skunk-works team members, peers and friends from The Signature Group/GE corporate days, "May the forces of goodness and light always shine upon you."

My former CMIT Solutions of Fox Valley North team members, including "Joe," a U.S. Special Forces veteran, and a man with indomitable spirit, who will never surrender. You trusted me, and allowed me to lead you, while we learned how to become an unstoppable Surging Team.

Thank you to Alan Weiss and his Summit Consulting Group, for challenging and equipping a new generation of consultants to pursue excellence in our craft.

To my wonderful editing and design team at Over and Above Press, Rick Benzel and Susan Shankin, thank you for helping me clarify, express and present the unique ideas that became the 10 BOLDskills for Accelerated Team Success. You kept me focused on my innovative team leadership ideas, and my book and message are immeasurably improved.

About the Author

All worthwhile things in this life are difficult.
They take money, time and energy. The outcome is never
certain. Make sure you live your life, lead your team,
and perform your work with no regrets.
Do incredible things, but also have some fun, as you
"tackle the thing that couldn't be done."
— SCOTT BRENNAN

Scott Brennan is the founder of BOLDbreak, Accelerated Success Experts. Our BOLD Purpose is to create a reliably repeatable methodology to help company owners and corporate team leaders create unstoppable Surging Teams. Our BOLDskills for Accelerated Team Success is that reliably repeatable team success methodology. Surging Teams have higher productivity, report higher levels of team member well-being, have less turnover, better health, and higher company profits. Your competitors will never see you coming!

Scott Brennan was previously owner and president of CMIT Solutions of Fox Valley North, a franchised technology company serving businesses in Chicago's Far Northwest Suburbs from 2006-2014. For 8 years, Scott ran his franchise business from his home-based office, before selling his business for a fair profit. During that time, Scott was able to participate in those critical family events that many corporate executives miss out on. While operating his CMIT business, Scott won multiple national awards: Rookie of the Year 2007, Breakout Franchise of the year 2008, Franchise of the Year 2009, President's Award 2011 & 2013, and Million Dollar Club Award Dec. 2013.

Scott was also a dean of the Pacesetters peer collaboration group, participated as a member of the franchisee advisory council to help advise CMIT's CEO, and gave a keynote speech on "franchisee survival" at CMIT's 2014 national convention in New Orleans.

Before purchasing a CMIT Solutions franchise business, Mr. Brennan worked for companies like Rewards Network, GE Financial Services, The Signature Group, MCI Telecommunications, and Time, Inc. Mr. Brennan earned his MBA from DePaul University's Kellstadt Graduate School of Business in 1999, and holds a Bachelor of Computer Science degree from Northern Illinois University.

While at GE, Scott led a skunk-works team that developed a breakthrough national dining program, Dining à la Card, which was eventually purchased by Rewards Network. Scott was awarded the "Chairman's Challenge Award for Outstanding Intrapreneurship" for this successful skunk-works effort. Now, fifteen years after the sale of our corporate division, our skunk-works team still tells our BOLD success stories that drive me to my knees with laughter, and smile with pride.

Most recently, Scott completed a continuing education certification in "Character Strengths at Work: Using Strengths to Engage Employees, Clients and Students," sponsored by the VIA Institute on Character, and accredited by the International Coach Federation.

Contact us

BOLDbreak, Inc. is an organization committed to helping entrepreneurs and intrapreneurs repeatedly equip their teams to achieve astounding success, through our BOLDskills for Accelerated Team Success Training, and become an unstoppable Surging Team.

- Please send your comments or questions about *The Surging Team* to Scott@thesurgingteam.com.

- For more information about our BOLDskills for Accelerated Team Success Training, or if you'd like to explore how we can help your company increase the success potential of your team, contact us at Scott@BOLDbreak.com.

If you'd like to have Scott Brennan as your keynote speaker at your convention, business event, or college, please contact us at Scott@BOLDbreak.com.

The 10 BOLDskills for Accelerated Team Success is now available in an exciting video format, which includes an interview style discussion and a walk-through of some exercises for each BOLDskill. The team leader can immediately use these and begin to apply them. The BOLDskills video series is a complementary media supplement to this book, but can also be used as a stand-alone training tool for corporate training departments. You can order the video training series from our website at www.BOLDbreak.com/videos or by sending an email to Scott@BOLDbreak.com.

www.ingramcontent.com/pod-product-compliance
Lightning Source LLC
Chambersburg PA
CBHW070350200326
41518CB00012B/2191